THE HOME WINEMAKER'S HANDBOOK

THE HOME WINEMAKER'S HANDBOOK

Philip Ward

Lyons & Burford, Publishers
New York

*To all my friends and co-workers in the wine industry for their tutelage and willing-
ness to share their knowledge. To my friend and editor Tony Meisel and his wonderful wife, Judi Olstein. To David Flood who has always been there. To my
friend, Bob C., thanks for getting me out of the woods and into the real world of
wines. And most especially to my father, P.H.W. III, and my grandfather, O.H.B.,
for introducing me into the wonderful world of wines. I thank you all and wish you
wonderful food and wine always.*

Library of Congress Cataloging-in-Publication Data
Ward, Philip, 1951-
    The home winemaker's handbook / Philip Ward
        p. cm.
Includes index.
ISBN 1-55821-303-1
1. Wine and winemaking—Amateur's manuals. I. Title.
TP548.2.W36 1994
641.8'72—dc20   93-42659
                                                            CIP

Produced by AM Publishing Services
227 Park Avenue
Hoboken, NJ 07030
Illustrations: Patricia Shea
Design: Tony Meisel

Printed in the United States of America

ISBN 1-55821-303-1

10 9 8 7 6 5 4 3

CONTENTS

To my wife, Paula Marie. She has been an incredible inspiration, and has been remarkably patient and helpful during the entire process. I raise a glass of great wine to you and your pursuits!

INTRODUCTION

Good wine is a necessity of life.
—Thomas Jefferson

Is there a better way to end the day than with a fine bottle of wine, good food and sparkling conversation among friends? This book will aid you in creating the wine portion of this exciting and enjoyable social exchange. It will also help you in understanding how to serve your wine and marry it with food. Wine has been a part of man's life before we recorded history and the first writings about wine appeared on stone tablets and papyrus. The Greeks are thought to have made wine as early as 1000 BC. Thankfully, winemaking techniques and practices have improved dramatically and now it is possible for anyone to be able to create very nice wine in the home. The technological improvements have occurred predominantly in the past 30 to 40 years and are due in good part to the scientists, oenologists and engineers based in the United States.

Philip M. Wagner wrote one of the most authoritative and innovative books on contemporary home winemaking in 1933 and even today it is still considered one of the best sources for the amateur. He certainly has influenced many budding oenologists to attempt new and daring experiments that have resulted in our advances in winemaking. These advances have made it very simple to make wine in the home. This book is organized to facilitate the making of wine in a very logical and straightforward manner. It will give the home winemaker the basic knowledge of equipment, types of wine, sources for grapes, juices and concentrates, the simplest way to produce wines of many styles, help you solve problems and many other important factors involved with winemaking.

There are numerous books and sources to aid you in your research into this fascinating subject and they will be found at the conclusion of this book.

Enjoy the process of home winemaking and revel in the results.

1
THE ORGANIZATION OF YOUR HOME WINERY

There is certainly no need to have your winery built up against a hillside and naturally control the environment but that would certainly be a dream for many home winemakers.

What the amateur winemaker needs is a working space that has access to the outdoors and also has a fairly constant temperature and humidity level. This temperature should be able to be regulated or altered during the fermentation and storing process. The work area should have electricity, hot and cold running water, be easy to maintain and be kept spotlessly clean.

Many home winemakers find that their garages, basements or small outbuildings work well as a base of winery operations. The winery should be organized in a way that works well for you and also takes into account the flow of the winemaking process. In an ideal situation there should be separate areas designated for the crushing and pressing of the grapes, fermentation of the must (juice), the aging of the wine, the bottling, the aging of the wine in bottle and also an area for the laboratory and sensory evaluations of the wine.

Should you have difficulty maintaining constant temperatures during the fermenting, cellaring or aging process, it may be necessary to have additional cooling or heating devices available for use. If you are planning to age your wine in barrels, it will be necessary to have a humid environment. You can augment the humidity of the area with the use of a humidifier or a dehumidifier, depending on the circumstances.

Floor drains in the home winery are also strongly recommended, as they allow for the ease of proper maintenance and cleanliness of the work area. The winemaking process can be very wet and messy, and these drains will give you the option of hosing and mopping the area very quickly. A well-maintained and clean winery keeps the possibilities of molds, bacteriological infections and general problems to a minimum.

2
WINEMAKING EQUIPMENT AND MATERIALS

Following is a list of equipment and materials that all home winemakers should own or have access to from a winemaking supply shop.

Five- and seven-gallon glass carboys: These are used for storage of the wine after primary fermentation and also for the long-term aging of small lots of wine. Plastic carboys are also available but they are a bit more difficult to work with, as they are not very transparent and it is good to visualize the progress of the wine.

One-gallon glass carboys: These are used for experimental lots of wine, trial blends or for use as aging containers for remainder lots that do not fit in other containers.

Hard plastic containers: The sizes available range from ten gallons to forty-four gallons. They are used for the primary fermentations of wine and are available with or without lids. It is recommended that you purchase lids if you are planning to make both white and red wines. The lid should be very tightly fitted to permit as little oxygen into the fermenting must. Some home winemakers use plastic sheeting as a cover and secure it with rope. Another vessel that is sometimes used by amateur winemakers is a used oak barrel. This can make an ideal primary fermenter for larger quantities of wine. Make

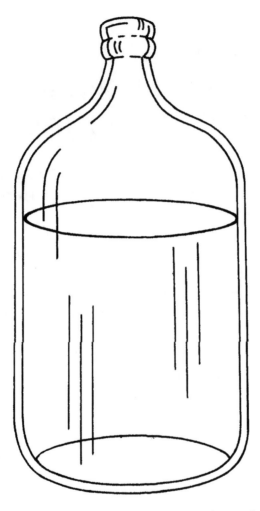

carboy or demijohn

sure that the barrel is in excellent condition, the staves and hoops are tightly fitted with no rust on the hoops, the barrel is very clean with no mold infestations and that the source of your barrel was not using it for a purpose other than the production of alcoholic beverages, preferably wine. The barrel should stand upright and have the top end cut off. The barrel could be coated with wax as well to keep the oak from imparting any flavors, or you could line it with heavy guage plastic sheeting. Some very dedicated and expert home winemakers will use new French or American oak as a primary fermenter for the production of Chardonnay and Sauvignon Blanc wines. More on this later in this section.

Plastic or stainless steel buckets with handles: Essential equipment in the winery for transferal of grapes, must, seeds, stems, skins, etc. and also to aid in the cleaning process.

Air locks/fermentation locks with white rubber stoppers: These locks are used in the fermentation process for white and red wines. They may be of plastic or glass construction and should

air locks

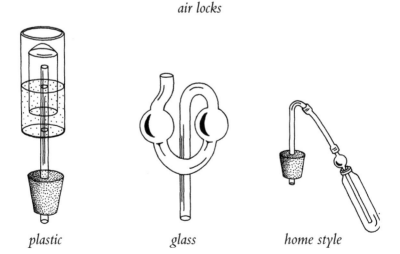

plastic   *glass*   *home style*

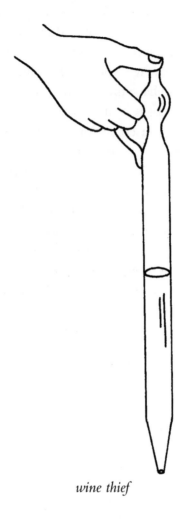

wine thief

have a white rubber stopper that fits snugly into the glass or plastic carboy. As long as wine is fermenting it is giving off carbon dioxide and this is audible by hearing a hissing sound and visible by the rise of bubbles in the fermentation container. This gas must escape from the container or there is a danger of possible bursting of the cork or, worse, the container. To leave a container open would allow the gas to escape but would also allow oxygen into the fermenting wine and this could cause discoloration and off aromas and flavors and also allow the admittance of vinegar-causing bacteria. The locks are very inexpensive and are essential pieces of equipment. Inside the lock is a cavity that contains metabisulphite solution that must be emptied and refilled every five to six weeks when in use. As long as fermentation continues, the carbon dioxide being produced can escape through the solution but once fermentation stops, oxygen cannot enter into the container. The lock also forms an excellent barrier to fruit flies and other bacteria.

Rubber or plastic tubing: For the transferal of wine from container to container or for bottling wine, this tubing is essential. Clear plastic tubing is suggested, as you are able to monitor the flow of the wine. There are also clamps and valves that can be quite useful in regulating the flow of wine. Valves are more expensive but they do not crimp the hosing, which leads to quick wear and potential damage.

The wine thief: This is a great tool to have, as it allows you the opportunity to efficiently and judiciously take a small amount of wine from the top of a container without disturbing the whole lot. An alternative is the home kitchen baster. Do not use this baster for any other function outside the winery and, as with the thief, keep it clean.

Funnels, funnel screens, measuring cups, measuring spoons: Funnels are useful around the winery for bottling, transferring small amounts of wine for experiments and tests and blending smaller amounts of wine. They come in many sizes and materials and it is best to have an assortment and it is recommended that you use food-grade plastic. Funnel screens are used to remove heavy or large particles from the wine and fit nicely into the funnels. Measuring cups and spoons are essential for adding certain material to the must or wine. Some of these include sugar, sulfur dioxide, acid adjustments and yeast.

Acid test kit: Having knowledge of the total acid of your must and wine is the best way to make the best-balanced wine that you can. The best way to test acidity is with an acid test kit. They are available for under $20.00 or up to $60.00. They are simple to use and come with easily understood directions. The process involves taking a measured amount of wine or must and by slowly adding measured amounts of an alkaline solution you can determine the acidity. As with all laboratory and winemaking functions, you must begin with clean, dry equipment. For testing the titration of a white wine or must, you will be looking for the change of the color from light green/gold to a light pink. This process will probably involve many small steps in the addition of the hydroxide to the liquid, which has been treated with an indicating liquid known as phenolphthalein, as the measurement should be very precise. For the testing of red wine or must, the process is a bit more difficult because of the darker color of the liquid. When first you add the hydroxide, you will notice a darker purple color that will disappear until the final titration has been reached. The wine or must will be a dark gray, and that is the stopping point for the test. After finishing the tests make sure that all the equipment is clean and that all lids on jars are well closed to insure that the hydroxide and the phenolphthalein remain fresh. You will determine the total acid of the unadulterated wine by the amount of hydroxide you used to achieve the color change.

Vinometer. This is used to measure the alcohol content of a finished wine. It is very accurate with dry wines but is less suitable for sweet wines. Vinometers work on the principle of surface tension, which varies with the strength of alcohol. Therefore, because sugar content interferes with this determination, you can see why this test does not work on wines with residual sugar. The instrument comes with directions for operation.

Hydrometer. The hydrometer may become your most important tool. This simple piece of equipment is capable of measuring the density or gravity of liquids, and has a number of functions it is able to perform to aid the amateur winemaker. A hydrometer is able to check the progress of fermentation, provide data from which the approximate alcoholic strength of wine can be calculated and also measure the natural sugar content of the must. The method in which this instrument is used is as follows.

A hydrometer jar is filled to within an inch of the top with either the must or the wine to tested. The jar should be about an inch wider and taller than the hydrometer itself to allow for the proper functioning of the test. As always, make sure all your equipment is clean and dry and in excellent working order. The hydrometer should be gently placed in the jar and pushed below the surface a couple of times to wet the stem. Spin the hydrometer gently to release any air bubbles that could give a false reading. After the hydrometer has come

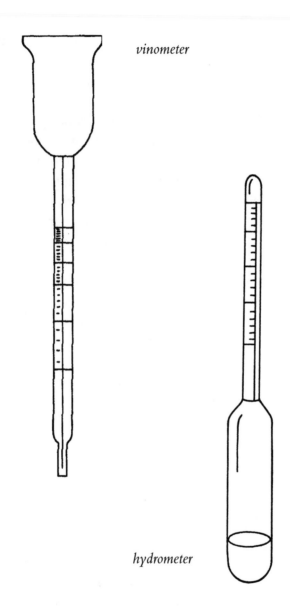

vinometer

hydrometer

to rest, look at the hydrometer reading with your eyes at surface level and judge where the stem emerges from the liquid. Do not be fooled by the slight curve, called the meniscus, which is formed by the stem breaking the surface tension and allowing the liquid to climb up the stem. Try to judge the exact spot where the liquid and the stem truly meet. The following table will show you the conversions that you should use in determining the results of your tests. It includes specific gravity, brix, the weight of sugar to be added to one gallon of must (if necessary) to achieve the alcohol or brix level, and the potential alcohol by volume.

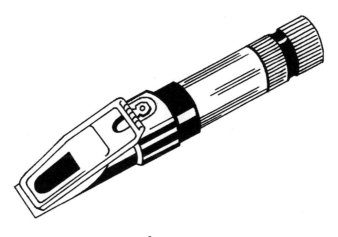

refractometer

Specific Gravity	Brix	Weight of sugar to be added to 1 gallon		Potential alcohol % by volume
		lbs.	ozs.	
1.000	0	0	0	0
1.005	0	0	1.7	0
1.010	2.4	0	3.5	0.9
1.015	4.0	0	5.2	1.6
1.020	5.0	0	7.0	2.3
1.025	6.25	0	9.0	3.0
1.030	7.5	0	11.0	3.7
1.035	9.0	0	12.7	4.4
1.040	10.0	0	14.7	5.1
1.045	11.5	1	0.6	5.8
1.050	12.5	1	2.7	6.5
1.055	14.0	1	4.7	7.2
1.060	15.0	1	7.0	7.8
1.065	16.5	1	9.0	8.6
1.070	17.5	1	11.0	9.2
1.075	18.5	1	13.4	10.4
1.080	20.0	1	15.6	11.2
1.085	21.0	2	2.0	11.9
1.090	22.0	2	4.3	12.6
1.095	23.0	2	6.3	13.4
1.100	24.0	2	9.0	14.0
1.105	25.0	2	11.7	14.9
1.110	26.5	2	14.3	15.0
1.115	27.5	3	0.8	16.4
1.120	28.5	3	3.5	16.9
1.125	29.5	3	6.3	17.6
1.130	30.5	3	9.0	18.0

For the home winemaker it certainly would be worthwhile to own two hydrometers, one that reads from 1.000 to 1.100 and another that spans from 1.100 to 1.200, enabling the winemaker to achieve the most accurate readings. You will probably have little use for the latter, as most musts or wine you are working with will fall below 1.100 specific gravity level. The only musts that will be above this level should, and most certainly would be, made into sweet or late-harvested-style dessert wines. Much more on these style of wines in an upcoming chapter. Potentially the most important function this inexpensive piece of equipment can perform is to notify you when the fermentation has been terminated. Some home winemakers rely on the tasting method but unless you are an experienced taster and have been involved with many winemaking sessions, this is not the recommended method. During fermentation, yeast is continually converting sugar into alcohol and carbon dioxide, which is altering the specific gravity of the liquid, and the level will decrease over time until it finally stops moving altogether. It is suggested that you check the fermenting must on a regular basis to determine when it has completed.

Refractometer: Not an essential tool, but can be especially useful for the experienced amateur who wishes to purchase fresh grapes. This expensive device allows you to measure the ripeness of a grape.

Grape press: The old traditional wooden basket press has been updated and works very well at extracting juice from grapes. The purpose of a grape press is to extract the juice from the grapes but you do not want to extract more than the free run and possibly the first press. The press is made up of three distinct parts performing specific functions: 1) a basket-like container constructed of wooden slats that holds the pulp. These slats are usually held in by metal hoops; 2) a screw-driven press/plunger that presses down on the pulp and grapes slowly and gently onto a plate at the bottom; 3) a reservoir to catch the juice as it exits the basket press and then hopefully, with some other material, guides the juice into a primary fermenter or other holding tank. There is also available a small press made of food-grade plastic that is very good for the amateur winemaker who is producing small amounts of wine. The cost is very reasonable.

A recent change has come about in the home-winemaking community and that has been the introduction of the small bladder press. This press has been in use on a commercial basis solely because the cost factor for the home winemaker was prohibitive and the technology was not available on a scale that would benefit the amateur. The cost of these new smaller bladder presses is still quite high but if you are trying to make very high-quality wines from the best fruit available then you might want to make the investment. The difference between the traditional basket press and the bladder press is the efficiency of extracting only the best juice, and it accomplishes this task very gently and effectively. Although the outward appearance of the press is very similar to the basket press, the interior is quite different. Inside is a bladder that, as it expands, gently presses the grapes against the outer walls, extracting the free run and sometimes with a bit more pressure the first press juice. To reiterate, these new bladder presses are expensive but the quality of juice is remarkable. Prices for presses range from under $100.00 for a basic basket press to over $1000.00 for a large-capacity (for the amateur) bladder press. You might want to keep in mind before you make an investment in a press that it will only be used during the harvest season. A potential way to defray the cost is to find another home winemaker who would be willing to share the press.

Grape crusher and stemmer. A grape crusher is another piece of equipment that will only be used during the harvest and winemaking season, and therefore the investment in this machine should be scrutinized carefully. The pressing of grapes is made easier and is more effective if the grapes have been lightly crushed prior to being put in the press. For the amateur working with small amounts of grapes, there are alternatives such as crushing by hand or by foot. If you decide to use a crusher, there are a few moderately priced ones available and they perform quite well. Prices for a basic crusher range from under $75.00 to about $200.00. These do not stem the grapes and you will have to perform this task manually. For the amateur wishing a combination crusher-stemmer the prices escalate rapidly depending on the size unit you desire. These machines remove the stems and leaves and crush the grapes, which is certainly beneficial for the winemaker who has purchased high-quality fruit. Prices start at around $300.00 for a model that can handle about a ton of fruit per hour, and the top of the line machine will cost close to $4000.00 for a machine that crushes and stems four tons per hour. Again, prior to making an investment in crusher or crusher-stemmer, try to defray the cost with the help of another home winemaker.

Oak barrels: For the home winemaker, oak barrels may be an extravagance but the results you are able to attain may make the investment worthwhile. In upcoming chapters we will discuss the advantages of oak. The sizes and prices for these barrels vary depending on the type of oak used in their manufacture. The most expensive and best oak is that which has its origin in France, and the next best is from the United States. If you decide to use oak barrels but are not making more than fifteen to twenty gallons of wine it might be best to use a product called Oak-Mor™. This product will be discussed later but the main reason not to use oak is because of the potential of oxidation in the wine. As mentioned above, prices vary for barrels and they begin at under $100.00 for a five-gallon American oak barrel and top out at close to $500.00 for French oak with capacity to hold sixty gallons of liquid. The good news is that barrels may be reused for up to four to five years before they give flavors to the wine. More later in the book.

Miscellaneous equipment: Following is a list of equipment that may not be essential for the home winemaker but it is certainly important to know that these tool are in the marketplace. If there is a need for the equipment it will be mentioned in the body of the text and please refer back to this information when necessary.

Bottle rinser/sterilizers: If you are planning to bottle your wine, which I hope you are, then a bottle rinser is necessary. It comes in a few model types from a basic model that attaches to a spigot to a deluxe model that sterilizes the bottles.

Bottle rack: This piece of equipment is a great tool to dry the bottles after rinsing. It is a basic design and it certainly could be easy to construct in the home tool shop using wooden dowels attached to a piece of wood on a base. Considering that the product on the market is quite functional and inexpensive, this may be a waste of energy.

Bottle corker: A very essential tool that is quite easy to operate and retails for under $100.00 for a good single-bottle model.

oak barrel

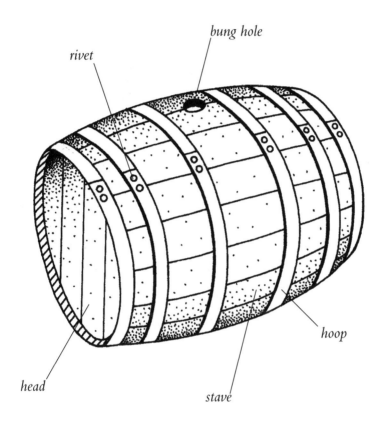

bung hole

rivet

hoop

head

stave

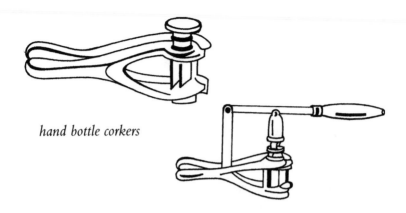

hand bottle corkers

Bottle and carboy brushes: These are excellent to have around the winery to remove sediments from the bottoms and sides and especially in hard-to-reach places. The handles are flexible and the brush is nylon.

Wine filter: Certainly not a necessary piece of equipment for the amateur. The filter system aids in cleaning up finished wine that may have particulate matter or a haziness.

Label attacher: For attaching your labels to bottles, this machine could be a great help. There is a very reasonably priced one on the market (under $100.00).

Sulfur strips and candles: These are for use by winemakers who are using oak barrels.

Miscellaneous test kits: Again, not all of these kits are necessary but they are certainly useful to have in the home winery.

Residual sugar test kit: There was at one time a kit called a Dextrocheck™ available but it is no longer available under that name. There is a good substitute named Clinitest™ that is used by diabetics. It is readily available and will work with wines with up to 5 percent residual sugar.

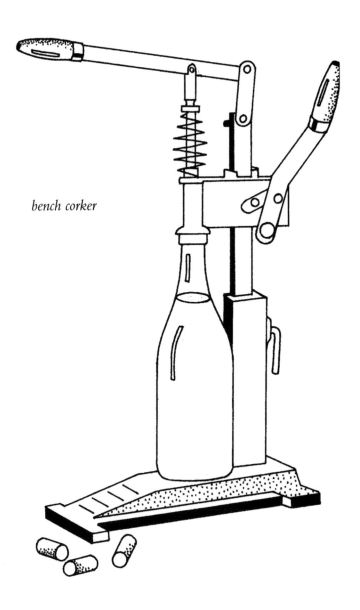

bench corker

Paper chromatography test: This is a test by winemakers to see if a wine, especially red wine, has gone through a malolactic fermentation. The test kit comes with all proper tools and instructions, and is available in either a vertical or radial style. The kits are priced below $50.00.

Sulfur dioxide test kit: This is a very good kit to have on hand, as there is very little worse than too much sulfur dioxide in wine. They are inexpensive, simple to use and have a shelf life of about six months.

Champagne corker, wire hood tightener and crown capper. These are essential tools for any amateur who is interested in producing sparkling wines.

3
TYPES AND STYLES
OF WINES

There are many different styles of wine that the home winemaker is capable of producing. The five main styles are dry red, dry white, rosé or blush, sweet white and sparkling. The winemaking process is essentially the same for all five styles except for sparkling wines, which incur a secondary fermentation in the bottle.

DRY RED

These wines are produced from red-skinned grapes that yield a pale juice (as almost all grapes do). The method for achieving red wine will be discussed in forthcoming chapters. The red grapes, juice or concentrates used for these wines include Cabernet Sauvignon, Merlot, Zinfandel, Pinot Noir and Gamay. The above grapes are known as *Vitis vinifera* and are grown only in suitable climate and soils. On the East Coast of the United States and in other less hospitable climates another type of grape has been developed, known as French-American Hybrids. Their principal red varieties are Baco Noir, Chambourcin, De Chaunac, Marechal Foch and Leon Millot. They are extremely winter hardy and also grow quite well in the warm humid summers typical of this area.

Cabernet Sauvignon and Merlot are the principal blending varieties in the French region of Bordeaux and also in California. They produce a sumptuous, full-bodied wine that exhibits aromas of cassis, blackberry, cedar, and occasionally

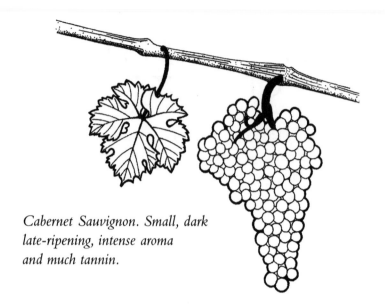

Cabernet Sauvignon. Small, dark late-ripening, intense aroma and much tannin.

mint and eucalyptus. The taste and flavors should carry over from the aroma, and the wine should also be dry with moderate to heavy tannins, with enough acidity to balance and enhance the fruit qualities.

These wines are best aged in French or American oak barrels (if you can afford them). If the wines are not matured in wood cooperage, they will taste simple and straightforward but because of the quality of the fruit they will still have a full-bodied taste and feel. John Parducci, owner and winemaker of Parducci Cellars in Mendocino, California, once remarked, "If I wanted wood in my Cabernet, I'd add toothpicks to my glass." John consistently made remarkable Cabernets that were redwood aged (redwood is a non-intrusive medium) and matured, in bottle, over a number of years into some of the most

*Merlot. Early-ripening
with good color and
softer flavor than Cabernet.*

beautiful wines in California. A true testament to the quality
of fruit utilized and John's winemaking abilities!

The history of the use of Cabernet Sauvignon in the Bordeaux region seems to date to the mid- to late-1700s, and its
use as the principal grape has grown dramatically, to the point
where it is the dominant grape. Cabernet can, as discussed
above, produce very full-bodied wines that can be very tannic
and robust. The Bordelais found that blending with other
grapes, such as Merlot, Cabernet Franc, Petit Verdot and
Malbec, the rough and tough Cabernet was calmed down and
smoothed out. There were other nuances added as well that

were and are positive attributes of the minor grapes. Some of those include a softness and forward fruit qualities from the Merlot, a slight herbaceousness and lean feel from Cabernet Franc, and blackberry qualities and fairly low acid from Malbec. When other vintners and winemakers began experimenting with producing Cabernet wines, they did not realize the beauties of the blend. Many California winemakers from the 1960s through the 80s insisted on crafting wines with just Cabernet, aged in either French or American oak barrels. Some of these wines are even now too big to consume, needing still more time in the bottle to soften the harsh tannins from the grape and the oak. Slowly winemakers from California and the world have come to the realization that Cabernet as a single variety can produce a great wine, but the best results come when one or all of these other varieties is blended.

Merlot, as a single variety has slowly but surely become a very popular wine in the United States. This popularity may stem from France once more, to a very famous Bordeaux producer, Chateau Petrus, from the little village of Pomerol. The wine has been coveted for many years by wine lovers from around the world, and it fetches exorbitantly high prices for its limited production. Chateau Petrus is almost 100 percent Merlot, and it is probably the wine that most winemakers are trying to emulate when working with this grape. Merlot, as mentioned above, has very forward fruit aromas of blackberry and cassis, and its softer tannins make it an ideal counterpart to Cabernet. Some winemakers are now blending a bit of Cabernet Sauvignon and sometimes Cabernet Franc to enhance the qualities of the Merlot grape.

Zinfandel (a.k.a. Zin) is thought to be America's only Vitis Vinifera variety, although much discussion has occurred as to

Zinfandel, unique to California, can make anything from a strong, full-bodied red to a light rosé.

its genealogy. Zin can produce myriad styles of wine, as exhibited by the simplicity of White Zin (see rosé) and the rich, full-bodied reds typical of most Zins produced today. The aromas frequently associated with Zinfandels include spicy, peppery, blackberry, cherry, jam-like and occasionally plum and mint. The flavors, once again, should be a carryover from the aromas, and the wine is dry with the fruit, tannin and acids in balance. These wines age very well in American and French oak, and also can perform nicely with no oak at all. Many winemakers find the use of American oak enhances the natural rusticity of this grape type and adds some wonderful aromas and flavors. Zinfandel is also a grape that does well when blended with other varieties and is capable of producing port-like wines. The very forward fruit aromas and flavors seem to work well with the necessary fortification to produce port-styled wine.

Zinfandel seems to grow well only in California but there are certainly experimental plots elsewhere, including Brazil (for White Zin.). The grape is thought to be related to or actually the Italian Primitivo grape and has some of the qualities of this grape. In Italy this grape doesn't produce very memorable wines and only in California, currently, does it produce wine of superior attributes. Zin's proponents believe that the grapes can produce wines equal in quality to the best Cabernets and Merlots. With age these wines show mature aromas of spice, cedar and berry that are quite similar to Cabernet. The grapes are, thankfully, available to the home winemaker, and the quality is usually good to very good. To emulate the style that is gaining in popularity, the home winemaker should, as always, buy the best fruit and age it in either American or French oak. This will bring out the best aromas and flavors Zin has to offer.

Pinot Noir (a.k.a. Pinot) is the principal grape found in the great red wines of France's Burgundy region and is considered the most difficult and fickle grape for most winemakers to produce great wine. It allows you no leeway, is extremely delicate and, from a viticultural standpoint, needs specific soils and climate to produce high-quality fruit. But when you make a good Pinot Noir, there are few, if any, better wines in the world. Pinot Noir's aromas and flavors are reminiscent of cherries, strawberries, strawberry jam, raspberries, occasionally plums and has a tendency towards earthiness, truffles, mushrooms and "gout de terroir" (flavors of the earth). Winemakers

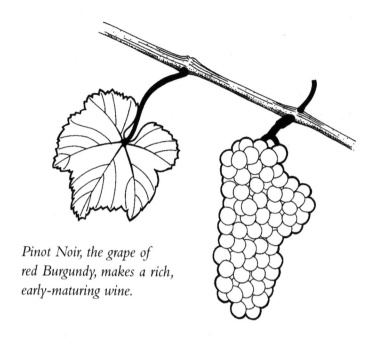

Pinot Noir, the grape of red Burgundy, makes a rich, early-maturing wine.

consider Pinot the Holy Grail of grapes and are constantly experimenting and refining their techniques. The style of wine typically produced is on the light side, but the wine has enticing fruit aromas and flavors, with the tannins and acids well balanced.

Pinot Noir can be a difficult grape for the amateur to locate, but the search will be worth it if you can find high-quality fruit. Pinot is grown throughout the world and it is finally gaining a foothold in the United States, Australia, and other countries in Europe. As described above, it is a very troubling grape to grow and from which to produce wine. It is very susceptible to diseases as well as rot and has hundreds of clones even in the tiny area of Burgundy. The vine is one of the oldest in the world and is thought to be one of the first cultivated from wild vines. Because of these multitude of clones, one is never sure as to the exact style of wine or the aromas and flavors the grapes will produce. In an ideal world, Pinot should be aged in only the best French oak and aged in these barrels for up to a year or more. The cost of the grapes, the difficulty in finding quality fruit and the cost of barrels will probably discourage most home winemakers from working with this most elusive grape.

Gamay is the principal grape of the Beaujolais region of France, and the wine produced is very fruity, light, delicate and dry. The exuberant fruit and delicate taste make it the ideal transitional wine for people unfamiliar with red wines. The aromas and flavors are of rosé petals, cherries, raspberries, strawberries and other berry fruits. The tannins are usually quite delicate and the acidity level is well balanced by the fruit. The longevity of these wines has always been questioned, but if you have ever tasted a five- to six-year-old well-made Cru Beaujolais, such as Moulin a Vent, there should be no answer to the question but a resounding yes! Most winemakers prefer to age their wines from this grape in non-intrusive vessels, to preserve the fresh-fruit qualities but the wine will pick up some nice qualities from oak that may be in its second or third year of use.

How many people really want to drink a rough and tough Cabernet or Zin? This is where grapes such as Gamay offer up their lovely delicate fruit qualities. The wines are even tasty in the dog days of summer, as they are very quaffable with a slight chill, and with the light tannins, they make a great match with spicy and grilled fruits. Although Gamay is best known in the Beaujolais region of France, it is planted as well in the Loire Valley area of France. In this region it produces a wine of similar characteristics to the Beaujolais version. In California there are some people who firmly believe that the Napa Gamay clone in use is not a Gamay at all but an inferior clone of the Pinot Noir grape. Even if it is, it still produces some very nice and delicately fruity wines. If you do happen to find some Napa Gamay available at the marketplace or locate a vintner willing to sell some, don't hesitate, as the potential wine created will be a joy to drink.

Although being used less, Carignan was one of the most widely used wine grapes by home winemakers because of its heritage and ability to make full-bodied, rich and high alcohol wines. It is also quite versatile in that it can produce a very nice rosé wine and makes a wonderful blending grape. Carignan has been in use for centuries and is thought to have originated in Spain but its main plantations were and still are in the south of France. It has a quite thick skin, which makes it ideal for the long travel across the United States for Eastern winemakers and, as mentioned above, makes fairly alcoholic and deeply colored red wines. It is known in America as the grower's grape because of its potential for high yields and ability to exist in diverse climate and soil conditions. Many growers and producers have found that with specific site selection, Carignan is capable of producing quite high-quality wines.

There are certainly other grapes that the home winemaker will occasionally run across for red-wine production. Grenache, which will be discussed in the rosé wine section; Syrah, the classic grape of the Northern Rhone Valley of France; Mourvedre, a varietal seldom seen alone and typically used in the Southern Rhone in a blend with Grenache (it is gaining in popularity, although plantings are limited, in California winemaking circles); and Barbera, which has been grown in

California for years and originated in the Piedmont area of Italy.

The French-American hybrid grapes also produce a wide variety of style and tastes of red wines. Chambourcin, Baco Noir, Leon Millot and Marechal Foch are the most often used to produce good red wine. They offer aromas and flavors similar to Cabernet and may also have a slight grassy and vegetal quality that can be very nice as a component in the finished wine. The tannins can be quite forceful at times, depending on the winemaking style, and the wines can do well when aged in oak cooperage if desired. For Eastern United States winemakers, these grapes are easily accessed, as they proliferate in almost all the states along the Mid-Atlantic region. Many wineries are willing to sell either grapes or juice/must to the amateur. Chambourcin has certainly received the most press and accolades for its abilities to make very rich and full-bodied wines that have structure, balance and fruit as well. Leon Millot has a following as well because it is one of the few grapes to have juice that is lightly pink in color and can make quite favorable red wine as well as a nice rosé.

DRY WHITE

These wines are produced from green-skinned grapes and offer the winemaker a diversity of styles from light, fruity and delicate to full bodied and rich. The dominate grapes for white wines are Chardonnay, Sauvignon Blanc and Riesling. These are all part of the *Vitis vinifera* variety and are the most widely available to the home winemaker. Other *Vitis vinifera* varieties will be discussed later. French-American hybrids are capable of producing wonderful dry white wine. Again more later.

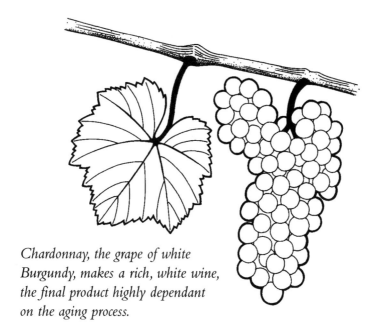

Chardonnay, the grape of white Burgundy, makes a rich, white wine, the final product highly dependant on the aging process.

All three of the above mentioned grapes make very distinctive wines with widely divergent characteristics ranging from grassy and light to tropical fruity and full bodied.

Chardonnay is the most revered of the white wine grapes and is the principal white wine grape of France's Burgundy region. The most expensive of these are Le Montrachet, Puligny Montrachet, Batard Montrachet and Chassagne Montrachet. The wines are produced from tiny vineyard sites with ideal soil and climate and the yields are restricted to produce only the best fruit.

In California, Australia, Italy, Washington State and even the Eastern United States, Chardonnay is much less expensive and can be a prolific producer of high-quality fruit and hence wine. It is a very forgiving grape from the standpoint of the winemaker, unlike Pinot Noir. Most winemakers find it quite easy to produce a very palatable to excellent Chardonnay with very few problems. Because of its abilities to grow well in many different climates and soils and to produce quality wines, the explosion of Chardonnay plantings worldwide has increased annually for the past few decades and does not seem to be slowing down. Another reason that this has continued is that Americans have taken a very strong liking to the tastes and flavors of the grape as well as the ease of pronunciation of the name. Most don't even realize that it is the same grape that produces their favorite French white wine, Pouilly Fuisse!

Chardonnay's typical aromas and flavors include apple, pear, citrus (lemon and lime), pineapple and tropical fruits. In the case of Chardonnay, in particular, the aromas and flavors may be altered and fine tuned with a brief time of juice and skin contact and also with the use of French or American oak as an aging medium. The oak aging seems to bring out vanilla, caramel and toast-like aromas and flavors that are nice additions to the fruit components of Chardonnay. The main drawback to the use of oak, as always, is the cost factor! Chardonnays produced in non-intrusive vessels are quite nice wines, as one really gets to taste and appreciate the true natural qualities of the grape.

Chardonnay traces its history to the Lebanese and Syrians and there is still a small amount of the grape cultivated there. It is thought to be a strain all its own with no relation to any other varietal, although for years it was thought to be related to the Pinot family, hence the wines labeled Pinot Chardonnay in the 60s and 70s in California.

Sauvignon Blanc (S.B.) is the principal grape used in the Bordeaux and Loire Valley regions of France to produce a

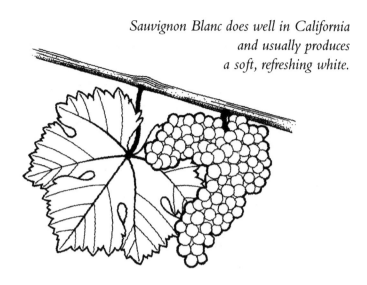

Sauvignon Blanc does well in California and usually produces a soft, refreshing white.

lovely dry white wine. The grape makes a lively wine with naturally high acidity and very appealing fruit flavors. Typically S.B.s have aromas and flavors of fresh cut grass, herbs, citrus, melon, flint, mineral and sometimes, unfortunately, cat pee. The beauty of this grape really begins to shine when paired with food. It performs so well with the lighter styles of cooking that are so prevalent today. S.B. has been grown for centuries throughout Europe but seems to produce the best wine in the Loire and also in Bordeaux, both for dry and sweet wine. It has spread rapidly into the new world of wine growing and has been readily accepted into California, South America, New Zealand and Australia. In each of these areas the style is essentially the same and the grape continues to slowly gain in popularity.

Sauvignon Blanc is blended many times with the Semillon grape. Semillon seems to add more body and richness to the delicacy of S.B. If grown in the proper soil and allowed to

---

ripen properly, S.B. can produce a wine that would benefit from oak aging, although most winemakers appreciate the wine that was fermented and aged in a non-intrusive container. The Bordelais are the main proponents of the use of oak-aged S.B., and the Californians are not far behind in this belief. Sauvignon Blanc is also a remarkable wine when it produces a sweet wine such as Sauterne.

Semillon, although not readily available to the home winemaker, produces very lovely and tantalizing wines. It is gaining in popularity in the United States, but S.B. still dominates the marketplace.

The Riesling grape produces some of the most delicate, floral and balanced wine in the world. Many people, unfortunately, associate Riesling with a sweet German wine. Assuredly they have never tried a Kabinett or Spatlese, which has the proper acidity to balance the fruit and sweetness of this grape. Home winemakers have decisions to make, as this grape produces wine of every level of sweetness from bone dry to unctuously sweet. Riesling aromas and flavors are perceived as being floral, tropical fruit, spice, honey, honeysuckle, stony, mineral-like and, when they are well aged, a petroleum quality that marries well with the primary aromas and flavors. Riesling is a grape that does not work well with any intrusive oak aging, as the gorgeous fruit aromas might be inhibited. Most German winemakers will age their Rieslings in stainless steel vats, German oak (non-intrusive) or some other medium. For the home winemaker Riesling may be the ideal grape because of its simplicity of use and the results it can bring.

Although Riesling is much maligned in the United States because of its perceived sweetness there is still a tremendous

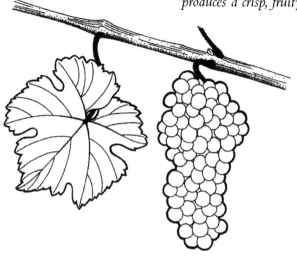

*Riesling, the grape of German whites,
produces a crisp, fruity wine.*

amount of German wine and American Riesling sold every year. Riesling will grow very well in many different soil and climate types, but it seems to produce the best fruit in cooler climates. The wines in Germany and the wines produced in the Finger Lakes region of New York State have very similar characteristics, and this is certainly due to their similarities of growing seasons and dormancy period as well. California has a very good track record with the grape, as does Washington State, and there is a style that is finally emerging in the United States after many years of experimentation. For the amateur winemaker, this style is quite simple to emulate, as it is crisp and clean with very forward fruit aromas and flavors. The Riesling fruit available to the home winemaker is usually very good, and this certainly helps to insure quality wine.

Other Vitis Vinifera varieties that are available include Gewurztraminer, Chenin Blanc and Semillon. These are cer-

---

tainly not widely available to the home winemaker unless you are lucky enough to live near a good vineyard source or do business with a company who stocks frozen juice. Gewurztraminer yields a very perfumed, spicy, lychee-nut-scented wine that has the potential to be either dry or sweet. Gewurztraminer is one of the principal grapes of the Alsace region of France, and is commonly thought of as producing sweet wines. In reality, 90 percent of the Gewurztraminer in Alsace is made bone dry, but because of its difficult to pronounce Germanic name, the misconception continues. If you do run across some nice-looking Gewurz., try to make a small batch in the dry style. Chenin Blanc makes wine with aromas of green apple, citrus and melon, and has very good natural acidity. Chenin Blanc is the predominant grape used in the Loire Valley region of France known as Vouvray, and makes either very dry wines or sweet still wines. This variety is also capable of producing very nice sparkling wines too. Chenin Blanc is also blended quite often to Chardonnay because of its natural acidity and flavor components. Chenin Blanc has been very popular with California winemakers for its ability to produce very nice dry table wine. Semillon, as discussed earlier, is blended with Sauvignon Blanc and as a stand-alone varietal can produce lovely dry wine that has superb balance and flavors. Aromas are reminiscent of citrus fruit, herbs, lanolin, melon and fresh figs, and the taste is crisp and clean with a very delicate waxy feel on mid palate. Semillon is the principal grape of the Bordeaux white wine production which is minuscule when compared to red wine production. Semillon when blended with portions of S.B. and sometimes Muscadelle makes incredible dry and sweet wines as well.

The two principal French-American hybrids used for dry

white wine production are Seyval Blanc and Vidal Blanc. These two have become synonymous with delicate fruity and dry white wines made in the Eastern United States. They are ideal when treated very simply and produce wines that taste great without any oak aging. Aromas are similar to those of Chardonnay and Chenin Blanc, and they also have a slight grassy component. These two varieties plus a few others are readily available to East Coast home winemakers and especially those living in the Mid-Atlantic Region. Most of the vineyards in the East are planted with these hardy white vines.

ROSÉ AND BLUSH

Rosé wines have long been popular in European winemaking communities because they brought the best of two styles together. The wine consumer has the flavors and aromas of light red wine and the crisp, dry, refreshing delicacy of white wine. Today commercial winemakers tend toward light, slightly sweet blush wines (with just a "blush" of color) that don't exhibit the beauty of true rosés.

Rosé wines are traditionally made from Grenache, Syrah, Carignan, Cabernet Sauvignon, Cabernet Franc, Pinot Noir and now of course Zinfandel. The method for making these wines will be discussed later but essentially the winemaker leaves the white juice in contact with the red-skinned grape for a short period of time. Another method is to blend a light and fruity red wine with a crisp and dry white wine. Rosé wines in the classic style have the aromas and flavors of the grape of production, are quite delicate on the palate, and have a refreshing crispness and a clean dry taste and finish. They are superb wines for summer consumption and marry well with warm-weather foods.

On the East Coast many winemakers are producing very nice rosé wines from the French-American hybrids, especially Leon Millot and Chambourcin. Leon Millot is popular because of its slightly pink juice and attractive fruit qualities. Grenache has long been the favorite of winemakers for the production of great rosé wines and unfortunately because of a few large American wineries, the name was almost ruined in the mind of the consumer of a generation ago. Thankfully, Grenache has begun to rebound from this bastardization and there is a small group of vineyardists and winemakers crafting really lovely versions of the classic dry rosé. For the home winemaker, trying to find Grenache outside of California and the West Coast may be difficult.

SWEET WHITE

Sweet wines are much misunderstood by novice wine drinkers. The conception is that all sweet wines are like the pop- and fortified-wine types available at inexpensive prices. To the knowledgeable winemaker and consumer, sweet wines, whether they be the late-harvest style or port type, are some of the most remarkably balanced and long-lived wines created. The degree of sweetness, known as Residual Sugar (R.S.) in the United States, may be as low as five percent to as high as 25 percent in special situations. The best results for late-harvest wines, be they from France, Germany, the United States, Italy, Australia, etc., seem to fall in the range of ten percent to 15 percent R.S. At this level of R.S. winemakers are able to achieve the balance of acidity to sweetness that makes these exotically sumptuous wines so appealing to dessert-wine lovers.

The principal grapes utilized for dessert-style wines are

Semillon, Sauvignon Blanc, Riesling, Gewurztraminer, Chenin Blanc, Malvasia, Muscat and, occasionally in the Eastern United States, Seyval Blanc, Vidal Blanc and Ravat. These wines are created by allowing the grapes to reach full maturity and ripeness, and in certain climates the grapes become infected with a mold called *Botrytis Cinera*. More on this "Noble Rot" later. With the grapes at their optimum sugar level, which is usually around 26–28 degrees Brix (measurement of sugar level) they also have very good acid balance. The aromas and flavors created by the grapes at this level of ripeness are certainly more concentrated, and they also walk a fine line of delicacy, as exhibited by most German Rieslings.

Botrytis Cinera, the Noble Rot, is a naturally occurring mold in most vineyards that is, almost always, kept in check by the vineyardists. In special cases when the soil, climate and grapes are at their optimum, the grape grower will allow the mold to spread throughout the specific area. The mold pierces the skin of the grapes and begins to slowly dehydrate the grape and concentrate the sugars. The wines from *Botrytis*-infected grapes are found to have aromas and flavors of honey, apricots, fruit blossoms, tropical fruits etc.

In Germany, there is a very special wine, Eiswein, that is produced from *Botrytis*-infected fruit that hangs on the vine until the first winter freeze. These wines are are rarely made and are considered the quintessence of dessert wine, as their acid to sugar balance is absolutely stunning. Some winemakers, unable to achieve winter freezes, have begun experimenting by taking their super-ripe grapes and freezing them either in a commercial freezer or transporting them to a frozen-food producer. The results have been quite favorable.

The true beauty of dessert-style wines really begins to show after a few years of bottle age and some have been in very drinkable condition even after a hundred years in bottle. The reasons for this are the high sugar levels and the beautiful balanced acidity that seems to hold the wine together and allows them to age gracefully.

For the purpose of this book we will concentrate on sweet white wines and not the Port wine style, but it is worthwhile knowing the method in which they are created. As in other dessert-style wines, they are made from very ripe grapes (traditionally from red-skinned grapes) and are allowed to ferment on the skins until proper color extraction and sugar levels have been reached. The fermentation is stopped by the addition of high-alcohol natural spirits, leaving the finished wine with an R.S. of eight to 12 percent and an alcohol level of 17 to 22 percent. These wines, whether they are produced from the traditional Portuguese varieties, or from Cabernet or Zinfandel, have a very full-bodied viscous taste and nice acid balance, and can be very long lived.

SPARKLING WINE

Champagne in France is the original sparkling wine and it is always made from three principal grapes, Pinot Noir, Chardonnay and Pinot Meunier. With the explosion in popularity of inexpensive sparkling wine from around the world, many new grapes have been found that can produce very nice "bubbly." Chenin Blanc (France), Semillon (Australia), Parellada (Spain) and Riesling (Germany) are just four varietals capable of solid-quality sparkling wines.

Grapes used to produce good-quality sparkling wines should, ideally, be harvested early, before full ripening has taken place. Most producers look for Brix levels between 18–

20 degrees. This allows for good acid levels and moderate fruit components. Sparkling winemakers wish to showcase the light fruit qualities combined with the typical yeast and bread dough aromas and flavors. The wine should jump onto the palate with good effervescence and finish very clean with a long, dry taste. Sparkling wines are made by a fermentation in a primary fermenter; then the secondary fermentation takes place in the bottle and is known as the *Methode Champenoise* (Champagne Method).

Chenin Blanc, Chardonnay and Riesling will probably be the most easily accessible grape for the amateur to locate in the marketplace as well as some of the French-American varietals. Chenin, the only grape permitted for sparking Vouvray (*vin mousseux*) in the Loire Valley, makes wonderfully fruity and crisp sparkling wine and develops nicely with moderate bottle aging. Riesling is the king of German Sekt sparkling wines, and the predominance of these wines is produced in dry to medium-dry style. The very forward fruit, spice and mineral qualities of the grape still shine through the yeast aromas. Chardonnay is certainly widely available and is the principal white grape for sparkling wines. Styles are usually perceived of as being quite dry, and the Chardonnay fruit aromas are commingled with the yeast aromas.

The history of the production of sparkling wine and Champagne is a long and somewhat provocative one. It is generally perceived that the process of the Champagne method and the development of the proper bottle and closure were all developed in the Champagne region of France. As always when dealing with historical facts, there are disputes and counterclaims. The sparkling wine producers in the Lanquedoc-Rousillon region of France claim they were the first to make sparkling wine similar to what we know now. Dom Pierre Perignon is considered the father of Champagne and is thought by many to have developed the method to make wines sparkle. In actuality, Dom Perignon developed the cork closure to keep the wine from exploding out of the bottles and the blending of different grapes from different sources to create a "house style" and constantly researched secondary fermentation. Another important historical figure is the widow Clicquot, of the Veuve Clicquot Champagne house, who discovered the method to clear the finished wine of the particles and sediment of the secondary fermentation. More on all of these methods and procedures in upcoming chapters.

Styles of sparkling wines range from very dry (Brut) to medium sweet (Sec or Demi-Sec) to sweet (Doux or Cremant). All of these styles are interpreted on a somewhat individual basis and on a national level as well. Each winery and country has a perception of what the style describes to their palate, but generally the above words are adhered to on a regular basis. Sparkling wines are very labor intensive and can be somewhat costly for the home winemaker, but with practice the results are rewarding.

4
GRAPES, JUICES AND CONCENTRATES

For the home winemaker grapes, juices and concentrate are the foundations on which their hobby is based. In the ideal world the home winemaker lives in an area that has access to vineyard sources, and considers commercial winemakers amongst his/her friends. For those people who can't buy fresh fruit or don't know winemakers, there are options. Many large metropolitan areas have available grapes brought in by rail car or tractor trailer from the wine country during the harvest season. As the popularity of winemaking and wine enjoyment have increased more diverse varieties of fresh-picked (two- to five-days old) grapes are becoming available through produce purveyors, farm markets and even from the vineyards.

If you do live in an area that does produce grapes, whether they are *Vitis vinifera* (European heritage), *Vitis labrusca* (native American), or French-American hybrids, try to cultivate a working relationship with a small winery or a vineyard and hope that they will be willing to sell you some fresh grapes or must. Almost all forty-eight of the contiguous states and Hawaii produce grapes of some type. Many small wineries and vineyards need help during the harvest season. Why not donate some time or work very cheaply to gain experience and for the potential opportunity to access fruit for your wine. You will learn about viticulture, vineyard management, winemaking and the best sources for the grapes you desire. Knowledge of all of the above subjects will surely benefit the amateur winemaker, and these people all share the same love as you and are usually more than willing to share their experiences and knowledge with you.

ANATOMY OF A GRAPE

Besides sugars and acids there are other chemical compounds that have a dramatic effect on wine character and quality. PHenolic compounds include pigments, either yellow or reddish, and tannins, a group of molecules that contribute to the astringency (drying quality) in red wines.

Grape berries usually consist of the skin surrounding the pulp and four seeds (typically). The stems, which hold the berries to the vine, contain bitter-tasting resins, tannins, and acids. Stems are usually separated from the grapes before and during the crush. The skin of the grape holds much of the phenolic compounds, including pigment and tannin (red-skinned grapes are very high in tannin) as well as the other compounds that give wine its myriad aromas, flavors and qualities. The seeds, at the center of the grape, contain tannins, resins and oils. Care must be taken during the crushing and especially in the pressing not to break the seeds open. The pulp surrounding the seeds is where many of the compounds that affect the quality and the character of the grape migrate during the ripening period.

The pulp is divided into three distinct zones. Zone 1 is the closest to the skin, Zone 3 surrounds the seeds and Zone 2 is logically in between 1 and 3. In a mature grape, Zone 1 is the lowest in acidity, Zone 2 is the sweetest and Zone 3 is the highest in acidity. Zones 1 and 3 will harbor some tannin and Zone 2 no tannin at all. As a group of grapes is crushed the first juice to emerge is called the free run, which originates in

anatomy of a grape

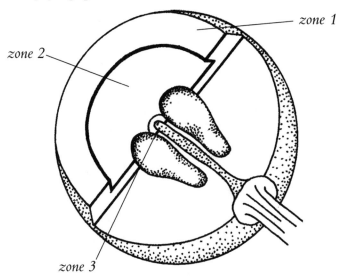

zone 1

zone 2

zone 3

Zone 2. This free run is the freshest, cleanest and purest and the preferred juice of winemakers. In optimum conditions, 60 to 75 percent of the juice to make wines can be considered free run. As more pressure is applied to the crushed grapes in the press, the winemaker begins to extract juice from Zones 1 and 3, with their added phenolics, acids and flavor components.

CLIMATE, SOIL AND VINEYARD PRACTICES

Climate, soils and, now more than ever, vineyard practices all have very special effects on grape quality and the quantity of grapes that a vine is able to sustain. The quality of the grapes a home winemaker uses is relative to the quality of the wine produced. With the myriad types of grapes, juices and concentrates available, it is necessary to find a consistent and proven

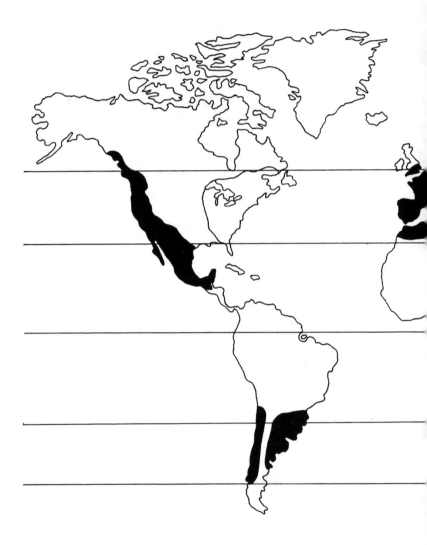

grape-growing regions of the world (shaded in black)

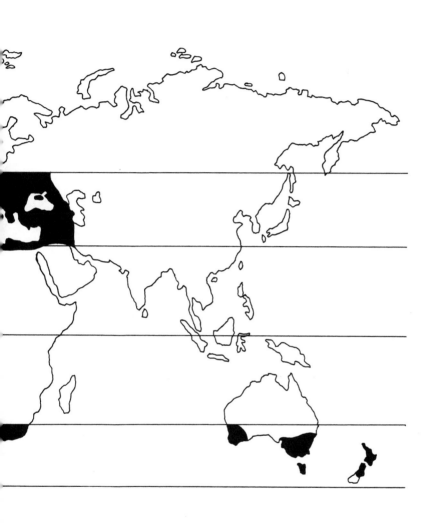

supplier of quality product.

No discussion of home winemaking would be complete without a look at where the grapes were grown and how soil, climate and vineyard practices can alter the quality of the fruit. If one looks at the map of the world, it is fairly obvious to even the novice winemaker or wine lover that there are definite climatic zones where grapes are grown. The delineated area seems to extend at its southerly end (of the Northern Hemisphere) at the 30th parallel in the United States and the 37th parallel in Europe to approximately the 48th parallel in the United States and the 50th parallel in Europe at the northerly extreme. In the Southern Hemisphere, the plantation is roughly the same and extends from the 40th parallel on the south to the 30th in the north. What all of these vast areas have in common is warm summer weather, which allows the grapes to ripen to their optimum levels, and cold winters, which give the vine a dormancy period necessary for rejuvenation. There are, of course, climactic differences year to year capable of altering the quality and the quantity of wine. These vintage vagaries are what make the difference between wines that will age for years and those that should be consumed quickly.

Temperature changes, rainfall and the lack of rainfall all have positive and negative effects on the quality and quantity of grapes available to the amateur as well as the professional winemaker. The quality of grapes is more important than the quantity and it has been definitively proven that as quantity increases the quality decreases. Most winemakers and vineyardists agree that the optimum quantity of wine grapes produced in a one-acre area is about three to four tons. This holds true for most Vinifera varieties such as Chardonnay,

Cabernet Sauvignon, Pinot Noir and Sauvignon Blanc. Some winemakers are pressing their vineyardists to restrict yields even more because they can see the difference in the quality of the fruit as it arrives at the winery and in the finished wine.

Specific soils can greatly affect wine quality, and this is being proven on a daily basis throughout the wine-growing regions. Certainly time has shown the Bordelais and Burgundians, in France, that the soils where the grapes grow in their regions are best for their high-quality wine production. This did not happen by accident; it took many years of experimentation to determine which grapes grew the best under these soil conditions. Vines, in general, seem to produce the best grapes from well-drained soils and soils that allow the vine to send out deep root systems. Too fertile a soil will yield a better quantity of fruit, and the quality will most assuredly be affected, as vines seem to produce the best grapes under stressful conditions.

Exposure to the sun is another important factor in the proper ripeness and quality of the grape. The predominance of the great vineyards in the world have excellent sun exposure and are typically facing in south-southeast direction. The early morning and midday sun appear to give the grapes the correct amount of sun exposure, and this increases the sugar content at an even rate. As the sun moves in its western arc and the grapes begin to cool down, the acid levels begin to stabilize, allowing for a balance of sugar to acid at harvest time. With this slow, even ripening of fruit, the winemaker is assured of superior aromas, flavors and components when the grapes are picked.

Vineyardist throughout the grape-growing regions are conducting dramatic experiments to find the best environ-

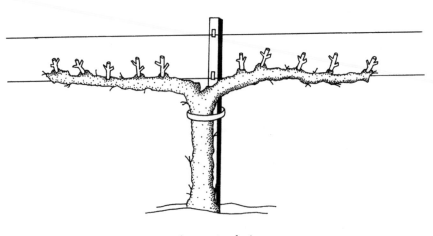

cordon-trained vine

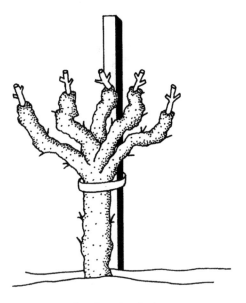

head-trained vine

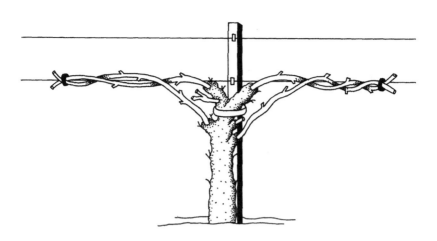

head-trained vine with pruned canes

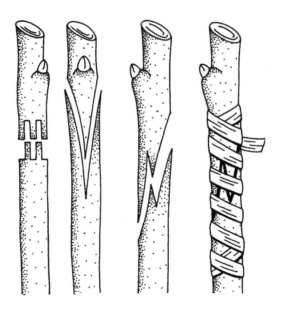

various grafting techniques

ment for their vines to produce the best grapes. Some of the experiments center around root stocks, vine spacing, management of the leaf canopy of the vine, grape cluster thinning, fertilization of the vineyard with organic matter rather than chemicals, pesticide and fungicide treatments, vine training, trellising and grafting techniques. Most winemakers are finding that grapes sourced from vineyards that are properly managed and cared for are of better quality.

Trellising systems and proper management of the canopy of leaves are becoming the hot topics in vineyards today. The canopy of leaves that spreads out from the vines is essential for the proper growth of the grapes. Many vineyard managers are finding that by controlling the amount of leaf canopy, the grapes are able to photosynthesize better, sugar and acidity levels are achieved at a more even pace, cooling breezes are able to flow through the vineyards, and less pesticide and fungus management are needed.

Organic farming practices is another hot subject in the world of grape growing, as it is in all farming communities. The American public is aware of the health benefits of a more naturally produced product. Many vineyards are slowly being switched to more organic methods of production, but this will take time as they have been farmed for many years using traditional pesticides and fungicides. Winemakers using fruit from organically farmed vineyards have been very happy with the resulting grapes, and the vineyard managers are finding that their cost of production is coming down as well. This return to organic, sustainable and bio-dynamic farming methods is definitely not restricted to America. There are literally thousands of grape farmers and wineries throughout the world returning to the methods that their ancestors were very successful with over the centuries.

The principal tenets of organic farming are the use of natural fertilizers, natural pesticides, natural fungus retardation and cover crops between the vine rows to add nutrients and create an environment for beneficial insects. Organic winemaking takes into account all of the practices just mentioned and adds to them. Most, if not all, organic winemakers will not use potassium metabisulfite in the winemaking process. They feel that there is no need for this chemical, and most wines naturally produce trace amounts of sulfur dioxide during the winemaking process that are enough to act as preservatives of color, and will restrict the potential of secondary fermentation. Experiments continue on this method of organic winemaking, as there have been some problems with certain of these wines having problems in the bottle. For the amateur it is recommended that they use as little sulfur dioxide as possible, but don't risk problems with your wine.

SEASONS OF THE VINE AND GRAPES

The cycle of the vine begins in the spring after the dormant stage of winter. During this dormancy period, when there is no sap running, the vine will have been pruned. During the early spring, as the sap begins to rise through the vine, it carries modest amounts of nutrients to the awakening vine. Five to six weeks after the sap begins to run, buds begin to burst out of the scaly wood that protected them all winter, and the canes and foliage develop from the buds. Unlike many fruits, grapevines do not send out foliage and fruit at the same time. Tiny, delicate leaves begin to form, and as they begin to grow, then the flower clusters appear. During the flowering period, which lasts about two weeks, the vine is very susceptible to weather conditions, especially late-spring frosts. Should the flowering be interrupted and not completed properly, the quality and the quantity of grapes could be severely affected. A classic example of frost damage is the 1979 vintage in the state of Washington. In that year the frost damaged many vineyards, including those used by Columbia Winery. At harvest time, the new winemaker, David Lake, realized that he had remarkable quality grapes from a few vineyard sources and he had the potential to make an extremely long-lived Cabernet Sauvignon. That wine produced from those very good grapes from a dramatically reduced crop was called MILLENIUM™, as David felt the wine would last until the year 2000 AD. The wine was and still is quite concentrated and is showing the potential to live up to its name. The result of this frost could have certainly been much worse for the grapes had the growing conditions after the frost been less than what they were.

After flowering is complete, a tiny green berry will appear, take form and eventually become a grape. During the summer months the grapes mature and grow in size. During this same period the foliage is growing and spreading out from the canes and is constantly being monitored for the need for pruning (canopy management). The vineyard manager is tilling the vineyard, fertilizing, spraying and thinning the grape clusters if they are overproducing.

The next stage in grape development is known as the "veraison" or changing of color. In red-skinned grapes, the green berry-grape turns a red-purple hue and the green-white translucence comes forth in the white-wine-producing grapes. Veraison usually occurs at the very end of July or the beginning of August in the Northern hemisphere. As the grapes become more ripe, the sugar levels naturally rise and the acidity levels lower. Finally comes the harvest season. The season varies for each variety and typically begins with the picking of the varieties that will be used for sparkling wines (the beginning of August in California) and finish with later-maturing red wine varieties (late September to October).

Once the grapes have been harvested, the vines remain untended until the fermentation has finished. The stems, seeds, skins, lees (dead yeast cells) and other organic matter are then returned to the vineyard to act as a natural fertilizer and mulch. And the cycle begins again with winter pruning!

GRAPES, JUICES AND CONCENTRATES

As discussed earlier in this chapter, the best source for fresh grapes is a local vineyard in close proximity to your home winery. There are some differences in harvesting techniques that the home winemaker should be aware of before purchasing grapes from a local vineyard. The best grapes are those that are hand harvested in the early morning or even before the sun rises versus grapes harvested by mechanical harvesters. These hand-harvested grapes are placed in 40-pound lug boxes that allow the fruit to remain as fresh as possible and also prevent the weight of too much fruit to begin the crushing-pressing process prematurely.

Most vineyards where you will buy your fruit will be of the size that they cannot harvest by machine nor could they afford the cost of a mechanical harvester. But should you run across mechanically harvested fruit, it is worthwhile to know how this operation is performed. Mechanical harvesters drive down the rows of vines and violently shake the vine and the trellising system. This knocks the grapes onto a conveyor belt, eventually transporting them into large bins. During this op-

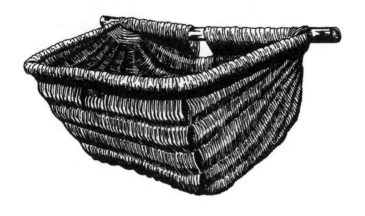

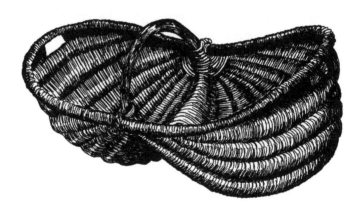

antique grape-picking baskets

eration, some of the grapes may be bruised or slightly crushed, exposing them to the air and beginning the oxidative process. To counteract this and reduce the loss in quality, many wineries have begun utilizing field crushers and begin the winemaking process in the vineyard. You can certainly visualize the problems that can arise for the home winemaker who purchases mechanically harvested fruit.

The optimum time to purchase your grapes is as early in the morning as possible and hopefully just as they are arriving from the vineyards. If you purchase fruit of this quality, you will be assured that the sugars and acids are at their proper levels. If the fruit is harvested too late in the day, the sugar level (Brix) will have begun to rise and the acid level to fall. If the vineyard owner will permit you, it would be perfect to pick your own grapes with some family members or friends, again insuring quality.

If you live in area that does not produce grapes for winemaking purposes, there are other means of procuring them. They will not be of the same quality level of those purchased from a local vineyard, but they will still make nice wine. Most major metropolitan areas have farm markets or fruit purveyors who annually bring in fresh grapes from vineyards, predominantly in California. These grapes are trucked in or sent by rail car, and are almost always refrigerated. If you find that they were not refrigerated, do not buy them!

The grapes purchased from these sources will probably begin arriving around mid to late August for the white wine varieties through September and possibly late October for the red wine varieties. The vineyard source for this fruit is usually California's warm, fertile Central Valley. Over 200,000 acres are devoted to grapes in this area which also supplies much of what we consume in the way of fruits and vegetables in the United States. The grapes from this area are certainly not of the same quality as those coming from Napa, Sonoma, Mendocino or the Central Coast regions of California due to the warm growing days and nights and the very fertile soils. Yields of six to seven tons per acre are not abnormal for Chardonnay, whereas two to three tons is typical in the other areas mentioned. As discussed earlier, the lower the yield the better the fruit. As with your vineyard contacts, develop a relationship with the purveyor and make him aware of your knowledge and desire to produce wine from the best fruit he has available. He may have fruit or sources for fruit coming from specific vineyards in better growing areas.

Fresh-pressed grape juice (must) is becoming more readily available as an alternative to fresh grapes. Two good sources for fresh juice are your home winemaking shop or a small winery. This juice is typically a combination of free run and first press that has had an initial treatment with sulfur dioxide to inhibit wild yeast fermentation and as an anti-oxidant. Treatment with sulfur dioxide is not essential at this point, but some wineries will add a small amount to protect the juice if it will be stored for a longer period than normal. The juice is refrigerated at around 33 to 36 degrees F. and allowed to settle before being sold. The quality of this juice will vary depending on the vineyard source and the grape variety. Buying juice that has been processed in this manner leaves out the crushing and pressing steps for the home winemaker and allows him/her to proceed directly to the fermentation process.

Frozen grapes and frozen juice are also becoming popular and more readily available. The only problem is finding a source that is willing to make the commitment to the proper temperature control for frozen product. The freezing process retains the freshness of the fruit and permits the winemaker to produce excellent-quality wine. Because of the freezing process and the quality of the fruit used, the cost of buying this product may be prohibitive to the small home winemaker. but prices are coming down and the quality of the fruit is exceptional. The typical quantities available are large drums holding 30 gallons and also five-gallon pails. The quality and variety of grapes available gets better each year. You can now find frozen grapes (red wines) and juices (white wines) from both California and Washington State's best growing regions. Almost every major grape is now accessible to the home winemaker, including the hard-to-find Gewurztraminer, Semillon and Mourvedre. I have even seen a "red field blend" that would allow the amateur to make an interesting version of southern French-styled wine such as Cotes du Rhone. These field blend styles have become very popular in commercial wineries, as they are light, fruity and fun to consume on a daily basis.

The use of concentrates is considered the easiest method for the home winemaker to produce wines. They are readily available at all winemaking supply shops, and produce five gallons of wine. They are sold in cans and bottles, and you should check with the retailer as to when they arrived in the store. The quality of the product will deteriorate over time if not refrigerated or at least stored at cool temperatures. Most concentrates are not dated, therefore it behooves you to find a retailer who is honest and seems to keep fresh stock on hand. Concentrates are available in many different styles of wine, and more single varietals are being made available. The single varietals such as Cabernet and Chardonnay are a bit more expensive, but they will probably produce a better wine than a "Chablis" that is a blend of who-knows-what type of grapes. I have recently seen a wide variety of grapes being offered in the concentrated form. The list included Gewurz., Riesling, Cab. Sauv., Trebbiano (Ugni Blanc in France), and an interesting blend of Cab.-Shiraz (Syrah), which is typical of Australia. This variety bodes well for the future of the concentrate market.

Concentrates are created by heating the grape must to the boiling point and reducing, under pressure, the liquid until only 20 percent remains. This evaporation concentrates all the flavors, aromas and phenolic compounds. For the novice winemaker, concentrates are a superb way to learn the winemaking process without all the worry of grape sourcing, purchasing tremendous amounts of equipment and the general problems of starting the process from scratch. To make the wine from concentrates, simply read the instructions on the container, purchase the basic equipment and follow the instructions or the recommendations of the retailer. The wine produced by the concentrate method will not be of equal caliber to a wine made from fresh grapes, but it will give you a nice learning experience and it will be fun to drink a wine you produced yourself. Wines made from concentrates are made for early consumption and occasionally may need some adjustments to their acid or sugar balance.

Remember that the process of concentrating this product does alter the quality and the primary aromas and flavors. Acids and other compounds will not be as they would be from fresh grapes. Also the grapes made into concentrates are probably not of superior quality, or they would have been sold as fresh grapes to a winery or made into frozen grapes/juice.

5
THE WINEMAKING PROCESS

Once you have sourced your grapes, juice or concentrate, it is essential to have your home winery in total preparedness for the winemaking process to begin. All of the equipment should be cleaned, sterilized (if necessary) and ready to accept the fruit and begin immediately upon arrival.

This chapter will discuss, predominantly, the use of fresh grapes, but if you are using frozen juice or grapes or fresh juice you may need to alter the process slightly. If you are using concentrates, it is essential to know the whole process even though you will not be performing all of the steps involved.

On the arrival of the grapes, the winemaker must crush and/or press (depending on the grapes used) them immediately to preserve their freshness. The gentle pressing will extract specific fractions of juice from the grapes. The free run juice is the juice that will naturally flow due to the pressure of the grapes on each other. Free run is considered by winemakers to be the best and clearest juice. The first press juice is extracted on the initial pressing of the grapes, and is usually combined with the free run, and these two together are what most winemakers use to create their wines. Second and third press juices are, if used at all, reserved for adjusting wines or for making "marc," a distilled product. In a commercial winery, the free run and first press are usually processed separately and then after the individual qualities have been identified, the

---

winemaker will create the final blend.

For the home winemaker using fresh grapes, it is recommended that they have access to or own a crusher and a press. The prices for these pieces of equipment range from moderately expensive to expensive depending on the quality and size you need. The essential task of these machines is to gently crush and press the grapes without damaging the fruit too much and not bruise the seeds, which would release harsh tannins and other unwanted characteristics. The old-time and current artisanal winemakers continue the practice of crushing grapes with their feet, understanding that you can feel the exact pressure necessary to release the best product from the grape. A good press is not as expensive as a crusher and is available in either manual or electric power. The manually operated ones are probably the best for the home winemaker, as you can feel pressure you are putting on the grapes. There is currently available a very good food-grade plastic press that has a stainless steel screw and it is very efficient and reasonably priced.

During the crushing and pressing, you will certainly notice that all the juice you are extracting is white/clear. There are only a very few grapes that have red- or pink-colored juice. Two of them are Alicante Bouschet and Leon Millot. Alicante is the old time Italian winemaker favorite because it produces very full-bodied, deep-colored and high-alcohol wines. Leon Millot is a French-American hybrid and is an early ripening variety that has pink juice and can produce rosé or deep red wines.

Skin contact before and during fermentation of red wines is essential for the proper extraction of color. The skins of red grapes is, as discussed earlier, where many compounds lie and also where red wine color is derived. Some winemakers are also finding that a certain amount of skin contact in white wine grapes, prior to fermentation, will release flavors and components that add a lovely complexity to the finished wine. Chardonnay and Sauvignon Blanc are the principal grapes being used and only a few hours of this contact is necessary.

Having finished the crushing and the pressing, proceed quickly to the fermentation stage lest the oxidative process could begin to deteriorate the quality of the must.

Wine fermentation, as with all fruit fermentations, is the process of conversion of sugar into alcohol by the use of yeast cells. When fresh grapes are brought into the winery, there are usually some wild yeasts that come along for the ride. These wild yeasts are typically not virile enough to complete a full fermentation, therefore almost all home winemaking today uses cultured yeast strains. Many commercial wineries use only cultured yeasts, but there is a movement among many wineries to use wild yeasts. They feel that you get more true flavor and phenolics in the use of the wild yeasts. The wild yeasts exist naturally in the vineyard, and also appear courtesy of the winemaker or vineyard manager fertilizing and mulching the vineyard with organic winery waste. The specifically cultured yeasts are available from the winemaking-supply shop, and are either in dry or liquid form. Two of the most popular yeasts are Montrachet, developed at University of California at Davis, and Epernay 2, developed at the Geisenheim Research Institute in Germany. Montrachet is a vigorous yeast that showcases fruit quality, whereas Epernay 2 is a slow-fermenting yeast, produces low foaming action and is preferred by Champagne and sparkling-wine producers. Another popular yeast is Pasteur Champagne, which is good for sparkling wines and also for stuck fermentations.

Before moving into a discussion of fermentation, there needs to be noted the use of sulfur dioxide during and after the process. Sulfur dioxide has been used for centuries by winemakers, fish processors and food processors to aid them in the production of their products. Sulfur dioxide inhibits the growth of wild yeasts and may also act as an anti-oxidant. The use of sulfur dioxide in the winemaking process is being trimmed down dramatically as winemakers find that they can do without it if the winemaking practices are rigorous and the environment is kept clean at all times. In this book, suggestions are made as to when to use it, and if you can get away with not using sulfur dioxide or at least limiting the quantities used, you will create a more natural and probably more complex wine.

DRY WHITE WINE FERMENTATIONS

Once you have finished pressing the juice from the grapes, and treating the must with a small amount of sulfur dioxide, it is recommended that you allow the must to settle for a period of time. This resting period will aid in the clarification and settling of any particulate matter. At this time you could also be giving the must some skin contact should you wish to do so. The skin contact should only last a few hours; then siphon the must off the skins into a new container. The settling process should take place in a non-intrusive container (a glass carboy is recommended) and the must should also be at a cool temperature (ideally 33 to 38 degrees F.).

After the settling period is over, siphon the clear juice off the settled particulate matter into a clean secondary fermenter, either glass, plastic or oak. Fill the container to about 3/4 to

5/6 full and inoculate with the yeast culture. The yeast culture should have been permitted to become active and also to rehydrate prior to this inoculation. If you feel it necessary to aid the fermentation, some winemakers will add a yeast growth stimulant/nutrient that contains nitrogen. This product is easily purchased from your winemaking supply shop. A common stimulant is diamonium phosphate and this, and any other one you might use, should be added at the time of the yeast inoculation. Cover the fermenter to keep flies, dust and especially oxygen out, or to a minimum.

Fermentation usually commences within 24 to 48 hours and may last from two to seven weeks depending on the Brix level at harvest, the type of yeast used, and other mitigating factors. If you should run a hot fermentation, which is not recommended, the fermentation will definitely take a shorter period of time. During fermentation it is suggested that as constant a temperature as possible be maintained. A cool fermentation of 55 to 65 degrees F. is ideal for retaining varietal characteristics and for preserving the fruit qualities. Some commercial wineries are reducing their fermentation temperatures even lower, and the results have been very positive. The problem for the amateur winemaker is lack of the proper equipment to accomplish this task and also the potential of interrupting the fermentation by lowering the temperature to the point where the yeast becomes inactive.

When you feel that fermentation is fully under way, you should monitor it carefully and check it to insure that it is continuing. If you feel that it has stopped and you have reached a point where the Brix level is at 0 degrees, check it with a Dextrocheck™, if you can find one, Clinitest™ or other similar test. Rack the wine off the gross lees (dead yeast cells) using a siphon, place into a clean secondary fermenter, fill as full as possible and close with an air lock. The air lock will allow for the escape of carbon dioxide, which is not desired in most dry white wines, and will not permit oxygen from entering the container. During this racking off the lees some winemakers feel the need for another minor treatment with sulfur dioxide or Bentonite to insure that fermentation does not recommence, because a small amount of yeast cells may still remain in the wine, and also to aid in the clarification process. If you decide to add Bentonite, the normal proportions are approximately two grams per gallon of wine. After two to three weeks the wine should be totally dry and it is time to rack the wine again. Rack into another clean carboy and fill to as high a level as possible, replace the air lock and permit the wine to rest for three to four months for a total settling and clarification.

The use of wood aging will be discussed in a future chapter but suffice it to say that the fermentation and the second to third stages of the settling could have taken place in oak barrels. This fermentation and aging would add very different flavors and aromas than when done in the inert glass carboy.

DRY RED WINE FERMENTATION

The fermentation and production of red wines is different than that of white wines. The main difference is that the juice is not pressed off the skins but remains in contact for color, tannin and phenolic compound extraction.

When the grapes arrive at the winery they are crushed gently and the stems are usually removed. During this gentle crush small amounts of juice will begin to run. The grapes and the juice are placed in a primary fermenter and treated

*punching down of red wine
in primary fermentation*

with a small amount of sulfur dioxide (in the neighborhood of from 50 to 100 ppm), then the active yeast culture and the yeast nutrient (if desired). Another precaution to take in red wine fermentation is the potential for the creation of hydrogen sulfide (the smell of rotten eggs). Some yeasts have a tendency to create this smell, and winemakers will add diamonium phosphate to the must prior to fermentation as a precautionary measure. If you smell any non-wine aromas during the fermentation, take immediate measures to correct the problem. Some winemakers believe in leaving the fermenter open, as the escaping carbon dioxide will keep out most bacteria and oxygen, which could be harmful. The cap that forms at the top of the fermenting must is a combination of skins and pulp and also acts as a bacteria and oxygen inhibitor. There are lids available for these fermenters, and it is worthwhile having them available.

Fermentation of red wines is usually conducted at a slightly higher temperature than for white wines. Temperatures of 70 to 85 degrees F. guarantee a positive color and tannin extraction as well as extraction of other compounds lying in the skins. If your fermentation gets out of hand and the temperature rises toward the 90 degree F. level, the yeast cells will become less virile and will not give the best results. As with white wines, try to keep the environment at a stable temperature, but should temperatures rise, pour cold water over the fermenting container to bring them down.

During the fermentation of red wines it is necessary to punch down the cap that forms on top of the must. This can be accomplished very simply by the use of a home potato masher or a sturdy spoon. As you punch down the cap, two to four times per day, you are recirculating the skins and pulp back into the juice, which provides excellent release of color and other components. In a commercial winery, the fermentation and punch down could last for up to 21 days, creating a very rich and full-bodied red wine with moderate to heavy tannins. Home winemakers will usually allow fermentation to continue for two to eight days and then press the raw wine from the skins and the pulp. The pressing of the wine, as always, should be gentle. This wine should then be racked into a secondary fermenter, topped up and closed with a fermentation lock. Try to retain some the wine for the topping up, which will be necessary over the aging period.

Before placing the wine in the secondary fermenter, many winemakers will inoculate the wine with a malolactic bacteria culture. This culture will induce a bacteriological change of hard malic acids to the softer lactic acids that are found in milk.

Now that all fermentations have been completed, the wine should be racked, using a siphon into a clean aging vessel for the slow maturation process. You should taste the wine and run any laboratory tests to see if any adjustments need to be made or any problems need to solved.

ROSÉ AND BLUSH WINE FERMENTATION

The fermentation of rosé and blush-style wines begins the same way as a normal red wine fermentation. The grapes that are typically used for these wines are Grenache, Cabernet, Zinfandel, Pinot Noir and Syrah. The grapes are crushed, the stems are removed, the juice and the skins go into the primary fermenter—these are treated with sulfur dioxide and inoculated with the active yeast culture and fermentation begins. Once fermentation has started, the winemaker must monitor the punching of the cap and the resulting color extraction very carefully. Most winemakers will pull off several lots with different color levels, fermenting them separately. This will enable them to ferment the lots to differing dryness levels and permit them to make a more balanced wine with a very attractive light red color. As the different fractions are pulled off they are pressed gently and placed in secondary fermenters, and air locks are put in place. Once fermentation is complete to the desired dryness level, the wines should be racked off the lees and placed in clean carboys. Most winemakers will add a mild sulfur dioxide treatment at this time to inhibit a malolactic fermentation. The crisp malic acids are essential to this style of wine.

If you wish to make a blush wine in the style of the commercially available wines, you should essentially proceed in the same method as above, the main difference being that most blush wines are extremely light pink in color, have a very delicate palate feel, a touch of R.S. (about one and one-half to three percent) and reasonably good acid balance. The difficulties for the amateur lie in achieving the light color and the proper R.S.-to-acid balance without the aid of sophisticated and high tech equipment. Commercial wineries use stainless steel fermenters that are jacketed with electrically controlled coolant. This coolant allows the winemaker to stop and start the fermentation when specific levels of color extraction and R.S. levels have been reached.

The different lots will be blended after a total fermentation has been completed. You can certainly visualize the difficulties for most home winemakers, who are accustomed to using cold running water to slow down a fermentation.

The best procedure may be to make a dry rosé or blush wine that is totally dry, and if you feel the need for a touch of R.S., you could add a touch of sweetened wine to the dry wine or add a sweet reserve, which is partially fermented wine. This will create a wine that emulates the style and flavors of commercially available wines.

SWEET WHITE WINE FERMENTATION

Sweet wine production is quite a bit more involved because of the ripeness of the grapes with which you will be working. There are inherent problems when working with very ripe grapes, and they will be discussed as we proceed through this fermentation process. There are basically three methods for producing sweet white wines. 1) If the winemaker is using fruit that is below 24 Brix, the common procedure is to stop the fermentation by cooling the fermenting must to slow the yeast down or to add approximately 250 ppm of sulfur dioxide to inhibit yeast production. The fermentation should be stopped at the desired R.S. level by the above methods. 2) If you are using fruit that has been infected with Botrytis Cinera, the Brix levels could be as high as 35 degrees. This fruit will be pressed and will produce limited amounts of juice of very high sugar levels. Once inoculated with yeast culture, fermentation will proceed slowly and will probably come to an end naturally and leave a luscious and rich, sweet wine. 3) The last method would be to use fruit with a Brix level in the 23-to-26 degree level, ferment dry and add a sweet reserve to raise the R. S. level. Sweet reserve is, as discussed in the rosé section, partially fermented wine that has had a sulfur dioxide treatment or has been cooled to halt fermentation and is then refrigerated for later use.

The problems inherent in very ripe grapes include the potential for oxidation because of their ripeness and also the potential for rotten clusters and grapes being included in with the ripe grapes. The longer grapes hang on the vine bunch, the more likely that grape rot will occur, and the longer the grapes take to arrive at your winery, the more likely that the oxidative process may begin. In choosing your grape source for a sweet wine, make sure the grapes are in as pristine shape as possible, and arrive at the home winery that way as well.

THE INCOMPLETE FERMENTATION
When the grapes arrive at the winery, crush and remove the stems, press lightly, treat with sulfur dioxide (moderate amounts), inoculate with an active yeast culture and begin the

fermentation in a fresh, clean carboy.

The yeast culture you choose should be one that works especially well with late-harvested grapes and has been developed to display the characteristics of dessert-style wines. Also be careful with the sulfur dioxide treatment, as you may want to add more as these wines tend to gain a more golden color and tend towards an oxidized look. Sulfur dioxide can aid in the proper color retention but do not oversulfur, as you may regret it later.

Once fermentation is under way, in the area of 60 to 65 degrees F., as with all fermentations, monitor it regularly to insure that it is proceeding at the pace you desire. Most sweet wine fermentations do not move along quickly due to the sugar content of the grapes but you should also be aware that sweet wine fermentations do have a tendency to stop because the yeast culture was not active enough or was the wrong type. In the event of a stuck fermentation and when there is still more sugar you wish to ferment out of the wine, add the must in small amount to fresh active culture until a strong fermentation has recommenced.

When fermentation has completed to the desired R.S. you desire, it will be necessary to lower the temperature to below 50 degrees F. to halt the yeast cell production and hence the fermentation. The best way to accomplish this is in an unused refrigerator or, if it is cold enough, stick the carboys outside. Once cooled I suggest you rack the wine into a clean carboy, adding about two to three grams of Bentonite per gallon and also about 75 ppm of sulfur dioxide. The Bentonite will aid in the fining and the sulfur dioxide will inhibit any yeast culture that might remain in the wine from restarting the fermentation. If for some reason the fermentation should start again it may be necessary to filter the wine through a filtration system. Unfortunately, most filtration systems are very expensive and certainly a few rackings and the use of paper filters may work for small quantities of wine.

BOTRYTIS-INFECTED WINE FERMENTATION

The chances and opportunity for an amateur winemaker to purchase and work with excellent *Botrytis*-infected fruit are very slim. Most commercial vineyards or wineries will leap at the chance to make these rare wines if given the opportunity and will be very reluctant to sell the grapes if they are in good condition. If you do have the chance to work with quality fruit, take it, but remember the care that must be taken and the cost factors involved. *Botrytis*-infected wines have a propensity towards volatile acidity and also browning and these can occur both during and after fermentation.

When the fruit arrives at your winery, examine it very carefully, checking for any other molds or rotten grapes that could ruin the final wine. Pick over the fruit painstakingly and retain only the best fruit and of course destem and destalk the fruit. Crush the grapes very gently, use only the free run and the first press and, if you desire, a small amount of skin contact can be quite beneficial to the end result. The best yeast culture to use is a Sauterne yeast, which was developed especially for the fermentation of these very sweet wines. It is available but you may have to do some research to find it. This yeast has the ability to ferment glucose faster than fructose, which is the opposite of most yeasts that are used for wine fermentations. Activate the yeast culture, rack the juice into a clean carboy, treat with sulfur dioxide prior to yeast inoculation to inhibit wild yeast fermentation, up to about 75 ppm, and then after the yeast is active inoculate the juice. An alternative to a glass carboy for the fermentation is the classic oak barrel. Traditionally in the Sauternes region of France new French oak barrels are the only medium used for fermentation, as the oak adds remarkable depth of character to the finished wine. This is another expense you should consider and it is also difficult to monitor the fermentation.

Once fermentation is under way, monitor it as carefully as possible, checking regularly for off aromas, stuck fermentation, color and any other problems. When the wine has reached the completion of the cycle and you feel the R.S. level is where you would like it to be, rack the wine into a clean carboy, add Bentonite and, if you feel it is necessary, a sulfur dioxide treatment and allow the wine to rest.

DRY FERMENTATION WITH
THE ADDITION OF SWEET RESERVE

For the home winemaker, this may be the best and simplest method of producing sweet wines. We discussed this process earlier in this chapter but be aware that there are other alternatives than the partially fermented juice/wine type of sweet reserve. Some winemakers will use juice concentrate, cane sugar, corn sugar and/or non-fermentable sugars such as glycerin and milk sugar. All of these materials come with positives and negatives; therefore it is worthwhile to perform some experiments or speak to knowledgeable winemakers about their results.

The process leading up to and through fermentation should proceed as it would for the production of a normal dry white wine. In the case of a dessert-style wine, you should use a grape that typically produces sweet wines like a Sauvignon

Blanc, Riesling, Chenin Blanc or Semillon. After fermentation has completed, rack the wine of the yeast into a clean container, add a fining agent, and allow the wine to rest. A trial blend should always be made before blending a lot of wine. When you feel comfortable with the trial lot, then complete the final blend. These wines should always have very forward fruit aromas and flavors, a delicate yet rich feel in the mouth and enough acidity to balance the sugar. After the final blend, allow the wine to rest in a clean carboy so that the blend will amalgamate and create a balanced finished product.

SPARKLING WINE FERMENTATION

For the purpose of this book, we will limit our discussion to the *Methode Champenoise* that was developed centuries ago and is still the only method permitted by law in the Champagne region of France. The other less-costly method is known as the transfer method or bulk method. In this method, the primary and secondary fermentations take place in large tanks and after the fermentation has finished the sparkling wine is bottled. The resulting wine is of good quality but does not have the overall aromas and flavors that are achievable with the traditional method. The Champagne method entails a great deal of work, commitment and certainly more money than the production of a dry white wine. There is also the time factor, as these wines can take up to four years before they are ready to be bottled. The extra dollars needed will be for the equipment and the heavier bottles necessary to contain sparkling wines, with up to seven atmospheres of pressure.

The fruit to be used should be harvested early, around 18 to 20 Brix, which will preserve the fresh, delicate fruit qualities and more importantly the acid levels. There are a few types of sparkling wines produced that the winemaker should be aware of: Blanc de Blancs (white wine from white grapes), Blanc de Noirs or rosé (a pink or rosé colored wine from red-skinned grapes) and wines that carry no designation (white wine from red- and white-skinned grapes). Blanc de Blancs are produced from Chardonnay grapes, but for the home winemaker, it could easily be made from Riesling, Chenin Blanc, Seyval Blanc, etc. Blanc de Noirs are produced from Pinot Noir and Pinot Meunier. And the blend on the undesignated wine may vary with the house style but normally is 60 percent red grapes and 40 percent Chardonnay.

For the home winemaker the simplest road to take will probably be to make a Blanc de Blancs (B de B), as there will be no need for a red wine fermentation nor for stopping fermentation and pulling off fractions as color extraction levels are met. B de B processing will begin as it would for any other dry white wine. The grapes are stemmed, crushed, pressed lightly and treated with sulfur dioxide. Try to use only free run and first press juice, and after the juice has settled for a period of time, inoculate with an active yeast culture. Use only an appropriate yeast that allows for proper fermentation and releases the best attributes of the wine. The fermentation should proceed slowly at around 60 degrees F.

After fermentation has completed to total dryness, rack the wine off the lees and have your Champagne-type bottles ready and absolutely clean. Inoculate the bottle with an active yeast culture, cane sugar and the wine. Cap the bottle with a crown seal and shake the bottle well to dissolve and mix the ingredients. Store the wine on its side in a cool, preferably dark environment of about 60 degrees. Every three to four days, shake the bottle to continue to mix the ingredients.

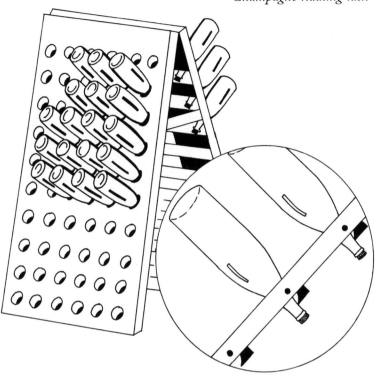

During this period of shaking the bottles, care should be taken because of the potential for exploding crown seals and the slow buildup of pressure as the secondary fermentation is beginning. The winemaker should wear gloves and some fashion of face shield, and should hold the bottle necks end down and away from the face and body. This process should be repeated for approximately two weeks or until you feel comfortable that fermentation is moving along. Then allow the wine to rest on the yeast. To check the progress, refrigerate a bottle for a few hours, very carefully open the bottle and check

---

the pressure released. If it seems as if it is developing nicely, recap the bottle and return it to its resting place.

The time the wine spends in contact with the yeast in the bottle is known as "tirage," and the length of time you allow is strictly up to you. Most winemakers find that a minimum of six months is necessary to release the classic bread dough and yeast aromas. As the wine stays on tirage, for up to four to five years if exceptional fruit is used, the aromas and flavors will become more intense and concentrated and the fruit will fade into the background. These aromas and flavors occur as the wine is in contact with the dying and dead yeast cells. The flavor and palate impression is of jubilant effervescence, and then the flavors of bread dough and fruit hit the mouth, followed by crisp acidity on the finish.

When you feel the time on tirage has been completed, then the "riddling" procedure must begin. There are specially designed racks for this process and also a very special technique to handling the bottles. The process should start with the bottles at the horizontal and should proceed over a few months to the point where the bottles are almost at the vertical position. Once the bottles have reached the vertical, the dead yeast cells and other matter will be at the crown cap end. During this procedure of riddling, the bottles are turned slightly and tapped quickly and with some force against the rack. As the bottles are turned and tapped, the particulate matter is released from the bottom and sides and the bubbles are fractured until they become quite small. If you are interested in seeing the difference between a good sparkling wine and a true Champagne, purchase an inexpensive bulk-method sparkling wine and a true Champagne. Open them and pour them into clean sparkling wine glasses and examine the difference in the effervescence and the size of the bubbles. True Champagnes will have pinpoint bubbles and a concentrated effervescence that starts at the bottom of the glass and streams upward, forming a light foam at the rim of the glass.

After completing the riddling it is time to prepare for the disgorging of the dead yeast cells and for the bottling. The only tried and true method to accomplish this is to freeze the neck of the bottle. To begin, refrigerate the wine, neck down, being careful not to dislodge any of the sediment at the neck, at about 45 degrees F. Next prepare a solution of calcium chloride and ice until the temperature is −10 degrees F. Place your bottle in the solution and let it remain there until a one-inch plug has formed. Open the bottle, with the crown seal up and the bottle at a 45-degree angle, with a crown cap remover. Aim the bottle toward a basin to catch the plug and the cap. Open the bottle, and the plug should fly out very rapidly. Quickly wipe the bottle top of excess yeast and other matter, then dose the wine with a sweet reserve if you want a touch of R.S. A touch will add a slight nuance to the wine. Many winemakers will have cognac or brandy as part of the "dosage" for extra aroma and flavor. Immediately cork the bottle with the cork and wire closure that is essential for this type of wine. Extreme care should be taken during this whole process, as there can be danger involved. It is also a very messy procedure, due to the amount of liquid involved.

The resulting wine should be allowed to rest to allow the wine to recover from the shock of bottling. The wine may be consumed over the next six months to three years, depending on the style and flavors you enjoy.

WINEMAKING

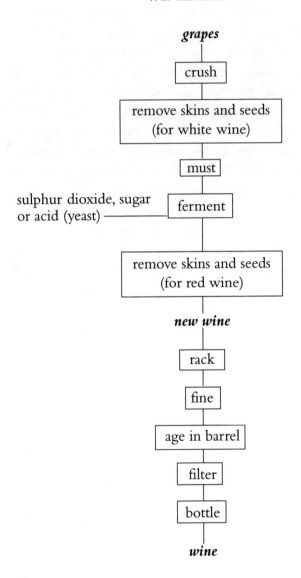

grapes

crush

remove skins and seeds
(for white wine)

must

sulphur dioxide, sugar
or acid (yeast) —— ferment

remove skins and seeds
(for red wine)

new wine

rack

fine

age in barrel

filter

bottle

wine

6
GENERAL QUESTIONS AND PROBLEM SOLVING

In this chapter we will try to answer some general questions surrounding certain techniques and to solve some problems that may occur during your winemaking.

What is malolactic fermentation?
Malolactic fermentation (a.k.a. M.L.) is actually not a fermentation at all but is a bacteriological change that occurs in many red wines and some white wines. In red wines it is a desired change but is usually only recommended in white wines with high malic acid content. This M.L. essentially changes the hard malic acids to the softer lactic acids. Malic acids are usually associated with green apples; they make our mouth pucker due to their sourness. Lactic acids are found in dairy products, and are perceived as giving a creamy effect on the palate.

M.L. is most often an induced process although it can occur naturally if a wine has not been racked properly. It is recommended that you induce this, as an M.L. from existing cultures will potentially not complete the whole process. If you are using wood or any other container for storage or especially for M.L., make sure that the container is very clean, as residual M.L. culture could still exist from a former use.

What are the molds most commonly found in the vineyard

and winery?

Molds can be beneficial or deleterious to grapes and to the winemaker. Certainly *Botrytis Cinera*, the mold that concentrates sugar levels, is respected for the wine it produces, but you certainly don't want it in a vineyard where you are growing grapes for dry-wine production. *Aspergillus Niger* and *Penicillum Expansum* occur in vineyards after rains, and both lower the quality of fruit and give the resulting wines off aromas. *Penicillum Expansum* as well as *Actiomyces* may be found in moist or still-wet barrels and the penicillum can also exist on corks.

There are certainly other molds and fungi that can exist and thrive in the home winery and may be damaging to the wines. The best answer is to use chlorine solutions and other sterilizing methods to prevent the growth of the molds or fungi. For wooden barrels that are not in use, keep them clean and dry and burn a sulfur wick/strip in them regularly.

What bacteria may cause problems in a wine?

The main problem-causing bacteria in the winery are acetic bacteria and can create wines with a vinegar-like component. These are not the same bacteria that produce true wine vinegars but offer similar aromas and flavors. The three main acetic bacteria are: *Acetobacter Aceti, A. Peroxydom,* and *A. Pasteurianos.* The typical aroma associated with the condition is that of nail polish remover. Be aware that these bacteria can take hold during a stuck fermentation and during the aging of the wine. Keep containers full, monitor fermentations and check the wine regularly. If you find that you have a problem and the wine is not too far gone, treat the wine with up to 100 to 150 ppm of sulfur and restart a fermentation. It is very difficult to mask these aromas and flavors; therefore it may be wise to discard the wine.

What is a stuck fermentation?

A stuck fermentation is one that never begins once the must has been inoculated or one that stops during the process of the yeast converting sugar into alcohol. The main sources of this problem are too weak a yeast culture, an inappropriate yeast for the style of wine or grapes, too much sulfur dioxide or too low or too high a temperature during fermentation.

Stuck fermentations, as discussed above, are potentially dangerous, as bacteria may enter the wine due to the lack of carbon dioxide that would normally be produced. Carbon dioxide acts as an inhibitor to air and oxygen that carry these bacteria. If a stuck fermentation occurs, the most advantageous way to restart is with a very active fresh yeast culture and also with the use of a yeast nutrient. If the problem was caused by too much sulfur dioxide, rack the wine immediately, allowing for aeration of the must and hopefully a dissipation of the sulfur dioxide, into a new container and restart the process.

How to correct problems of clarity

As discussed previously, most wines will naturally clarify themselves by the law of gravity. Many problems of clarity are caused by particulate matter that will eventually precipitate to the bottom of the container in. The other causes for haziness or cloudy wine include proteins, pectins, metal salts (calcium, iron, and copper) and yeast or bacteria cells. Most of the fining materials that are available at the wine shop will correct and resolve the lack of clarity in your wine.

The most traditional and still-used fining agent is egg white. Egg whites are used for red wines, and have been very successful for centuries, as they do not strip the wine of the characteristic aromas, flavors or tannins. The egg whites (one to two per large barrel) are whipped vigorously until frothy and slowly poured into the container. The egg whites form a curtain that slowly begins to precipitate through the wine to the bottom. As they fall the proteins in the whites latch onto any particulate matter and pull them along to the bottom.

Other fining agents include Bentonite, gelatin, isinglass (fish protein) and Sparkalloid™. Each of these agents performs the same function but some work better on specific problems. When using any of these, be careful, as some, such as isinglass, can strip color, flavors and even tannin if overused.

Along with fining, filtering can also aid in wine clarifications but should only be used in the most dire circumstances. Filtering is expensive because of the equipment involved, and also has a tendency to strip wine of character if not handled very carefully. There are currently some moderately priced home winemaking filtration systems available but they are normally not necessary for the amateur who has patience and racks and fines the wine well. See the last page of this chapter for more on fining and filtering.

What are and what causes off odors and flavors?
Off odors and flavors are surely the sign that there is a problem in the winemaking process. Once your olfactory and taste evaluations become aware, these components are easily detectable. This will only take time and a willingness to taste and evaluate all kinds of wines whether they be sound or have problems.

One of the more common odors found in wine is that of hydrogen sulfide and other sulfur compounds. These are most prevalent in white wines, and appear because of an over use of sulfur dioxide, stuck fermentations, the use of copper sulfate to prevent mildew in vineyards that usually have overripe grapes, and lack of the proper control of the air that reaches the wine. The aroma or odor associated with this is typically related to that of rotten eggs. If you find this problem the best way to try to correct it is to rack the wine into a clean container and during the racking vigorously splash the wine to aerate it and hopefully dissipate the smell. If you are not successful on the first attempt try it again in a week or so but at the end add one crushed Campden tablet per gallon. Fining and filtering as a last measure can possibly help, but if this aroma does not fade, discard the wine.

Volatile acidity (V.A.) is a common problem in red wines, causes a prickly feeling in the nose when inhaled and may also have that lovely nail polish remover aroma. As discussed earlier, this problem is caused by Acetobacter; once you have V.A., it is difficult to remove and if let go can cause a spoilage of the wine.

Adjusting tannin levels in wine

Because you are making wine on a small scale and are using either concentrates or less than the best red wine grapes, there may be a need for adjusting the tannin level in the wine. As you know, tannin comes from the grape skins and stems and from oak aging. If you find the need to adjust tannin levels up, the simplest way is to add grape tannin, which is available from the wine supply shop.

Mix the grape tannin powder with a small amount of experimental wine from the container. Allow a rest period for the tannin and wine to incorporate themselves. Taste the blend and adjust if necessary. Your wine shop owner may be able to give you some direction as well.

If you find that a specific lot of wine is too tannic, the best way to adjust this is to blend with a lot which is a bit softer or to fine the wine. Probably the best fining agent for this procedure is egg whites, but you could use any fining agent that you feel will work.

Adjusting acid levels in wine

Acid is certainly one of the primary components in wine and adds to enjoyment of wine, as long as it is in balance. Without acidity wines will seem to be flabby on the palate, will lack character and will not be long lived. Lack of acidity in red wines will contribute to the fallout of color over time. Wines lacking in acid present a problem at the table, as acidity helps to cleanse the mouth of rich fats, proteins and carbohydrates. If the acid level is too high in the wine, it will seem very sour and will overpower the fruit and many other pleasurable characteristics of the wine.

When the grapes, juice or concentrate arrives at the winery, it is recommended that you determine the total acidity (T.A.) of the wine. If you know your T.A. prior to the fermentation and you find a need to adjust the level up, add the proper amount of acid blend crystals to the must prior to starting fermentation. Be aware that acid levels will fall during and after fermentation about .05 to .20 percent, and you should always add the acid blend prior to the fermentation. Knowing the pH of the wine will aid you in determining the acid level, as there is a direct correlation between acid and pH levels.

The ideal range for pH for dry table wines is between 3.1 and 3.5. As pH level increases, the acid level will fall and vice versa. The decrease of acid level and increase of pH may cause bacterial problems, less stable color and less crisp, tart flavors.

If after the fermentation has finished you find the acid level too low, the adjustment should be made after the first racking has been completed. Use either the acid blend or malic, citric or tartaric acids. As with any blending or problem solving, make a trial blend in a small lot before the final correction is completed. If the acid level is too high after fermentation, an M.L. could be induced that would soften the hard acids. Another method to lower the acid is the addition of water to the must, which will reduce the level of acidity and increase the volume of finished wine. The disadvantages of this method are 1) the wine is lighter in style and has less positive attributes, and 2) the total acid reduction is really not as great as it seems to be.

Another method of lowering acidity is by cold stabilization. This entails adding cream of tartar to the wine, shaking or stirring to mix well, and storing at between 20 to 30 degrees F. for up to two weeks. You should shake or stir daily for the entire time to insure the proper mixing of the cream of tartar. After two weeks, allow the wine to rest for a few days and rack the wine of the tartaric acid solids that have precipitated to the bottom of the container. The difficulty for the home winemaker is finding an environment that has a constant temperature for the length of time necessary.

What is Brix and why is it important?
Brix is generally perceived as the measurement of sugars in grapes, but it is quite a bit more than that. It is actually the

measurement of soluble solids in grapes, must or juice. Sugars found in grapes are fructose and glucose, and normally constitute up to 90 percent of the soluble solids. Other solids include color pigments, glycerols, especially in red grapes, and minerals, proteins and pectins.

Degrees in Brix also helps in determining the amount of alcohol that can be produced in the final wine. There are easily available formulae that will aid the amateur winemaker. Degrees in Brix also aide in deciding the T.A. and the pH. It is generally believed that as Brix increases, T.A. will lower and pH will rise due to the ripening of the grapes.

Is it necessary to fine and/or filter your wine?

Not to belabor the point, but the less you use of any additive to your wine, the more natural it will be. Any of the fining agents mentioned in this book will work well to clean up your wine. The best method to clarify wine is through the racking process, and under normal conditions clarity will come with time. If you find that you have a clarity problem that will not remedy itself, then by all means use a fining agent.

Filtration of homemade wines is certainly a last resort, as there should be no need for this if your wine is sound and reasonably clear. Filtration is most frequently used by commercial wineries and very serious amateurs due to the cost factors involved. Filters are expensive, and most home winemakers can get good results with patience and fining if necessary.

7
AGING, BLENDING AND BOTTLING

AGING YOUR WINE

In previous chapters, we have discussed the process of fermentation, fining and filtration. Another central pert of the process is the aging of the wine prior to bottling. The aging regimen will aid the clarification of the wine and may make the need for fining and filtration unnecessary. During the aging the particulate matter and any cloudiness fall to the bottom of the storage vessel and eventually dissipate. Aging wine will also give the wine time to amalgamate all the aromas, flavors and the essential phenolic compounds that create a fine bottle of wine.

There are two types of mediums, discussed earlier, for the aging of wine. The non-intrusive type includes glass, older oak barrels (German, French, American and Yugoslavian), redwood barrels, stainless steel, enamel or glass-lined containers and concrete vats. Most of these are certainly not available to the amateur, and you will most likely be using glass carboys for the aging. Intrusive mediums are only made from French or American oak barrels from specific forests, and have seen no more than four to five years of use.

Aging your wine after fermentation has been completed does entail some preparation of the wine and the medium. All the containers should be very clean and dry and should not emit any off aromas. Any container that was previously used for wine storage should be cleaned well and inspected for any bacteria or fungus that could cause major problems in the wine. The wine to be placed in the aging medium should have been racked off its primary and secondary fermentation lees except when you want to lees age. The wine should also have been checked to insure that the fermentation process has completely finished, and this can be determined by any number of tests mentioned earlier. If the winemaker is making a sweet-styled wine there will certainly be a small amount of R.S. left in the wine and steps may need to be taken to insure that a secondary fermentation does not occur.

The larger the container you use to age your wine, the better. The size will allow for a slow, even maturation of the wine and will let the wine clarify easily. It is difficult to age wine in containers of less that five gallons, as the potential for oxidation and reduction of volume is greater and certainly can cause problems. In any aging process it is necessary to monitor the volume of the wine in the container and to top up the container with wine of the same type on a regular basis. Make certain that the container you are using has a closure that is as airtight as possible to keep the oxidation and volume reduction at a minimum. Keep your aging wine in a cool and humid environment and limit the light that enters your aging area to minimum amounts. Many wineries age their wines in underground or mountainside cellars, as they have the ideal temperature and humidity for the slow maturation of the wine. In a recent visit to France and Germany, all of the wineries we visited had underground or hillside caves that were shrouded in molds from the extremely humid and cool environment. There learned experience has taught them well.

As you are checking the wine for the reduction of volume

in the container, you should also be monitoring the development of the wine. If you begin to detect off aromas and flavors, remedy them quickly. If you find that the wine has reached the stage of maturation and amalgamation of aromas and flavors that you desire, bottle the wine.

NON-INTRUSIVE CONTAINER AGING

The predominance of home winemakers will use glass as their aging medium. There are also food-grade plastic containers. These containers typically come in one-, five- and fourteen-gallon sizes and are readily available at the supply shop. The one-gallon size is, as discussed earlier, not recommended for long-term aging but makes an ideal size for experimentation and also for wine used for topping up. Fourteen-gallon demijohns are a bit large for many amateurs but they make great containers for making a final assemblage of different lots prior to bottling.

Almost all white wines, rosé and some red wines should be aged in non-intrusive containers. This will preserve the fresh fruit qualities of the wine and allow the true nuances to come forth. Working with glass carboys and demijohns is ideal for the amateur, as the closures for them are very airtight and allow for very little oxidation and reduction in volume. If you are unable to fill the container to the top, you could lay a blanket of nitrogen gas on top of the wine. This gas is inert and will not affect the wine, but will actually protect it from any harm due to oxygen that may have been left in the space between the wine and the top of the container. Nitrogen is readily available in small cans, as it has become very popular with wine lovers as a way to preserve a bottle of wine that they were unable to consume at one sitting. The nitrogen will have to be replaced as a blanket on the wine every time you open the container, and it will also dissipate within a week or so even if you don't open the container. Some commercial winemakers will sparge their containers with carbon dioxide to insure that it is clean, and also will use it as a preservative and a barrier to oxygen. Carbon dioxide may also add a very lively and pleasant palate feel to the wine as long as it is used judiciously.

Once you have performed all the necessary tasks to insure that you have healthy containers and healthy wine, the only thing to do is be patient. As Orson Welles used to say when pitching Paul Masson wines on television and in print ads, "we will sell no wine before its time." This is certainly true for almost all wines. They need time to develop.

Lees, as discussed in the fermentation chapter, are the dead yeast cells and other sediments. Many winemakers over the centuries have found that aging their wines on the lees will add complexity and interesting nuances to the wine. In fact, in the Loire Valley region, which produces Muscadet wines, the best wines are perceived as being those that are aged on their lees, and they are labeled as such to distinguish themselves as being superior in quality. Aging wines on their lees, and in rare cases lees of another wine, can be problematic for the amateur and even the professional. The lees can contain components that will give the wine off aromas and flavors and may cause the wine to become spoiled. One of the main problems is that when a wine is fermenting, hydrogen sulfide is produced, but it can also occur when the dead yeast cells are beginning to decay. In conclusion it may be advisable to avoid lees aging unless you feel very adventurous or have the aid of someone experienced with the procedure.

If you have made the decision to produce a sweet white wine with a small amount of unfermented natural sugar, it is recommended that you rack the wine a few times to insure that the lees have been removed. If you are unsure of this prior to putting the wine into the aging medium, it may be necessary to add a small amount of sulfur dioxide to insure that fermentation does not recommence. The use of sulfur dioxide should always be kept to a minimum.

OAK BARREL AGING

Oak is most assuredly the premium aging material for wines today as it has been for centuries. Oak, whether it comes from France or America, is certainly expensive for the amateur but it offers a multitude of aroma and flavor components to the finished wine. The proper oak for the proper wine is very site-specific. The best oak is white oak, and originates in five French forests: Limousin, Troncais, Alliers, Nevers and Vosges. Over the centuries and with much experimentation, winemakers have found that each type of oak adds specific qualities to the wine. Some oaks have a tighter grain, others a looser grain. The white oak in America that is recommended for aging comes from forests in Missouri and Arkansas. It has been found through many experiments that the way the barrel is constructed has an effect on the wine.

The wood from the oak tree must be handled very carefully and specifically treated to make the best barrels. After the wood has been cut into barrel staves, they must be air dried for a minimum of a year, according to most experts. After drying, they are formed, by either steaming or heating over a fire, into the proper shape by the cooper. Before he closes up both ends of the barrel, he will char the inside of the barrel to the specifications of the purchaser. The charring of the barrel has three main designations, called "toasts": light, medium and heavy. This charring differs from the burning that takes place with the bourbon barrels familiar to residents of Kentucky and aficionados of Kentucky bourbon. These American oak barrels are, interestingly enough, shipped to Scotland for the aging of Scotch whiskey. The difference of the level of toast is a decision the winemaker will have made for each varietal he is planning to age in barrel. As one would think, the heavier toast level will give the wine more dramatic aromas and flavors. The air drying of the oak seems to soften the harsh flavors and tannins whereas kiln drying does not, as the wood is not exposed to the elements.

The American winemaking community has adopted the practice of using French oak as fervently as if it had invented its use. There have been companies created in the heart of Napa Valley that specialize in the manufacturing of French oak barrels. They ship the aged oak staves direct to the valley and there they are assembled by French- and American-trained barrel coopers. These barrels are made to the specifications of each winery, and the results of these new ventures have been quite successful, as the quality of workmanship is equal to that which comes from France. American oak barrels are gaining a very strong following among winemakers wishing to bring out certain more rustic, fragrant aromatics and oakier flavors. Zinfandel, the Rhone varietals and even some Chardonnays, from as far away as Australia, are being aged in American white oak barrels.

Aging in oak for the home winemaker will be time consuming, and the risk for problems to arise is very high, unless caution and preparations are made for the proper care of the barrels and the aging environment. The cost can be high, as you can see from the time and process that goes into constructing a quality barrel. The other cost factor that needs to be considered is the life span and effectiveness of the barrel. Most oak barrels will lose their ability to impart aromas and flavors on the wine within three to five years. The first year of use will give the strongest effect on the wine, and this will depreciate over the following years until you will finally have a barrel that will be a non-intrusive medium for aging the wine.

Oak is also a high-maintenance aging medium. After wine has been removed from the barrel, the barrel must be thoroughly cleaned of all residue, including lees, sediment and tartrates (tartaric acid solids that will form on the inside of the barrel). Clean the barrels with cold water (as it removes the least amount of extract from the barrel) and a solution of sodium carbonate (if, after cleaning the barrel, you detect moldy or off aromas. Mold or bacterial infections, as we have learned, can be deadly to wine. If after cleaning with the sodium carbonate solution you still detect problems, remove the barrel from the winery quickly and hope that the problem has not spread to any other portion of the winery or containment vessels.

Maintenance of the barrels also includes ensuring that they do not dry out when not in use. If the barrels should dry out, there is a risk that the staves will begin to separate and the hoops, which hold them in place, will begin to lose their effectiveness. The recommended way to prevent these problems from occurring is to keep the barrels filled with wine (sometimes a difficult chore for the home winemaker), or alternatively filled with a solution of water, sodium dioxide and citric acid. Keeping wine in the barrel is, of course, the best method, and is quite cost-effective, as the barrel will be in almost constant use. Should the decision be made not to keep a liquid in the barrel, it will be necessary to burn a sulfur wick or strip in the barrel. These strips should never be burned in a new barrel or in a whiskey barrel that has never been used for wine. If you have purchased a whiskey barrel, rinse it very well, fill it with water, let the water remain overnight and rinse again. Then burn a sulfur strip or wick in it. These strips will keep bacteria and molds from producing in the barrel, but if there is a mold in the barrel you will know it right away when you lower the strip into the barrel. The strip will go out when it comes in contact with a moldy barrel. The strips cannot correct a problem; they can only prevent problems from arising. If you have determined that the barrel is clean, lower the strip/wick into the barrel, attached to a slim piece of copper or aluminum wire. Lower it as far into the barrel as possible without it touching the sides or bottom and put the bung (plug) into the hole at the top. If you are planning to keep the barrel empty for more than two months, it will be necessary to rinse the barrel every sixty days or so and repeat the strip/wick burning procedure.

When you are ready to use the barrel again, you must rinse it thoroughly to insure that there are no residual effects from the strip/wick burning. This procedure, if not followed, could cause problems with hydrogen sulfide in the next wine put into the barrel. Once the barrel is rinsed, check the staves and hoops for any problems, fill the barrel with water and allow it to rehydrate for twelve to twenty-four hours. Check it regularly for leaks. If any appear, take it to an expert or, if you can find one, a cooper.

Aging wine in barrels will also require a strict regimen of topping off the wine. Because oak is a porous medium and not airtight, there will be a reductive and oxidative process taking its course during the aging. Most winemakers check their barrels weekly and top them up whenever necessary. You can now see the need for smaller vessels of the same wine. During this inspection it is recommended that the winemaker also smell and taste the wine to see how it is progressing and to assure that no problems are arising. After topping is completed, replace the bung in the barrel very tightly as you normally would. For most home winemakers, wine loss may be greater due to the use of smaller barrels and lack of the perfect environment that commercial wineries have available to them. The topping process should continue on a weekly basis for the first few months and bimonthly thereafter.

Lastly, should you decide to age in barrel, it is recommended that you inoculate the wine with a malolactic cultures, as this fermentation (bacteriological change) could start naturally and not run its course without the aid of a culture. Some winemakers want to retain the high acid in their white wines and will take the risk of not inoculating. For all red wines it is recommended that this inoculation take place. A controlled ML is better than one that could cause future problems.

OAK CHIPS, OAK EXTRACT AND OAK-MOR™

For many home winemakers, these are the logical alternatives to the high cost factor and high maintenance of oak barrels. They are all very inexpensive and readily available at supply shops. Their use is very simple and the results, if not exactly the same as true oak aging, are very good, and when used properly the resulting wines taste great. Many commercial wineries have certainly been the forerunners of the development and use of these products. For them, retaining a price point and quality level in the marketplace are paramount, and they have found that the judicious use of these products will give them excellent results. Each wine you make will differ slightly, and the amount of ingredients you use will differ. The best answer may be to try experimental lots until you come up with the final product you wish.

AGING DRY WHITE WINES

As discussed in the fermentation chapter, once the wine has completed the fermentation, it is suggested that you add a fining agent to aid in the clarification process. This certainly is not an essential step, as the wine will probably clarify naturally if you take the time to rack the wine properly and remain patient with the process. The use of a fining agent is not the artisanal way of winemaking, and with the movement toward natural winemaking it may be better to stay clear of fining unless absolutely necessary. When aging your wine in any medium, it is an individual taste that will determine the time to bottle. Only experience with the aging process will dictate when to remove the wine from the vessel and begin the bottling. The longer you age a wine, the more homogeneous the blending of aromas, flavors and phenolics will be. The non-intrusive or inert vessel will give you the purest components of the fruit and will highlight the fruits qualities.

Whether you are using Chardonnay, S.B., Seyval Blanc, Riesling or any other white variety, the primary factors you are searching for are balance of fruit, dryness, sweetness, acidity and the overall impression the wine leaves on the palate.

Aging the wine too long will begin to mute these characteristics and therefore it is prudent to monitor the wine closely. If you find that the wine has flaws such as high acidity, then it is recommended that you blend in a portion of wine with a low acid balance.

If you decide to age your white wine in oak cooperage, be aware that the fruit qualities will be altered. Oak in combination with white varietals, like Chardonnay and S.B. (the most commonly aged in oak), will add a vanillin, caramel and sometimes toast-like character to the wine. There also may be a perceived richness and sweetness in the wine, as the wine extracts certain phenolics from the wood. Due also to the oxidative and reductive properties of oak, flavors and aromas may become more concentrated, and these will certainly occur in a first-year barrel. If using a new oak barrel, it is recommended that the wine remain for only a few months, as there is chance that the fruit qualities will be completely dominated by the oak. The wine produced in this style will potentially, with age, show very little fruit and will taste like the barrel it was aged in previously. A prime example of this, on a commercial level, was the new wave of California winemakers in the late 1960's and 1970's who, in emulation of their French brethren, aged their wines in oak. Unfortunately, they did not have the knowledge or the experience, and many of their wines, after a few years of bottle age, had completely deteriorated into wines with no fruit, lots of oak and very little acid. They have certainly learned their lessons well, and the quality of wines currently available show a judicious use of oak. One of the main things they learned was that a combination of new and second-, third- and even fourth-year oak worked much better in crafting a great wine.

AGING DRY RED WINES

What has been said previously about white wine aging holds true for red wines as well. When using inert mediums for aging, the fruit qualities will be preserved and the wines will taste fresher and lighter on the palate.

The aging process for red wines, whether in non-intrusive or intrusive containers, will be a longer process. This is due to the ML change that is suggested and also because red wines do take longer to amalgamate all their components and create a fine wine.

We have discussed earlier the fining procedure for red wines and the materials that could be used. As with white wines, fining is not essential, as the clarification will occur naturally by frequent rackings. Also the natural tannins and proteins in red wines will speed this along during the aging. It may take longer than an aided fining, but the resulting wine will be more natural and will certainly taste better.

To aid the clarification, it is good to rack the wine a few times immediately after fermentation and also to rack the wine during the aging time. During the racking, keep the wine as free of oxygen/air exposure as possible. This can be accomplished by using a siphon hose or a pump and gently pulling the wine off the precipitated matter at the bottom of the container. Besides aiding the clarification, the racking will soften some of the harsher tannins in the wine, and also, if done carefully with minor splashing of the wine into the new vessel, it will aerate the wine. This splashing will allow the aromas, flavors and phenolic compounds to become more forward and will hopefully let them marry well. These rackings should continue over the course of the aging but should decrease in their frequency the longer you age the wine. Rackings should always be with the cleanest possible materials, including the siphon hose, pump and containers. If you are aging the wine for up to a year, you need only rack the wine every couple of months after the initial rackings during the first few months. After these rackings you will probably have no need whatsoever for fining or filtering the wine. Don't forget as you are racking the wine to be monitoring the fill level of the container and also the progress of the wine. Topping up is, as always, important to keep the reductive and oxidative process in check. The container should always be tightly sealed.

Oak-aged red wines are definitely more complex and seem to age longer and more gracefully than wines aged in non-intrusive mediums. The judicious use of wood will add to the tannin level and balance and will bring out other nuances in the aromas and flavors in red wines. Each grape type will speak to the winemaker as to the length of time it should remain in barrel. If you feel that the wine has reached its peak in the barrel but is still lacking in some areas, you can remove it to a non-intrusive vessel to complete the aging period.

Just as in white wines, red wines can become over-oaked, aggressively woody and too tannic for the fruit quality. Remember that balance is everything, and that if a wine has too much of any one factor it will dominate on the palate. There is nothing worse than a red wine that has tannins that rip the mouth apart, leaving a very astringent and mouth-puckering feel. The fruit, tannins and acid need to be in balance if the wine is going to age gracefully.

AGING ROSÉ AND BLUSH WINES
The aging of these wines, prior to bottling, is certainly the shortest period of any wine you might produce. Blush and

rosé wines are to be consumed over a very short time, and they do not improve in bottle. If anything, they begin to deteriorate over a period of a year or more in bottle. The light color extraction will begin to fall out in the form of particulate matter, and the exuberant fruit aromas and flavors will become more muted. Although some people enjoy a rosé with some bottle age, these wines are most appreciated in their youth. The best way to tell if a rosé/blush wine is beginning to deteriorate is that the color will become slightly orange and there will be a slight haziness in the bottle or glass.

There are very few people who will age their wine in anything but a non-intrusive medium. Why waste the money on oak that could completely alter the pleasure of the fruit qualities in this style of wine? When fermentation has completed, rack the wine off the lees a few time over the period of a week or so to aid in the clarification, and remember to keep air exposure to an absolute minimum. Place the wine in an airtight container and monitor it regularly for problems, topping if necessary and progress. If you feel that it is necessary you could use a fining agent for this style of wine. The time in the aging container will be an individual choice, and most winemakers find that a few months is optimum for the marrying of flavors and preservation of fruit.

AGING SWEET WHITE WINES
Most sweet white wines are aged in non-intrusive containers. The only exception is the aging of wines based on the Semillon and Sauvignon Blanc grapes. The classic example of this is Chateau d' Yquem from the Sauterne region of France. This wine is actually barrel-fermented and also barrel-aged only in new oak! The resulting wine is spectacular and is also one of

the most expensive wines in the world. The chances of the home winemaker ever seeing fruit of this quality are virtually nonexistent, and you should use only non-intrusive containers. Some German winemakers have experimented with French oak aging on their Rieslings, and have found that it inhibits the fresh aromas and flavors that are the credentials of this grape. They usually prefer their centuries-old German oak uprights and now stainless steel.

After completion of fermentation, rack the wine off the lees, and add a fining agent if you desire or allow the wine to clarify by the racking process. During the first few months of aging, rack the wine a few times, monitor the progress, check the fill level, top up when needed and check for adjustments or the development of problems. Most sweet wines need up to six months of aging before they should be bottled, and some winemakers will allow the wine to rest for up to a year. Remember fruit, sweetness and acidity need to be preserved, so do not overly age your wine. If it is ready, bottle it and it will certainly continue to develop in the bottle.

AGING OF SPARKLING WINES
The aging process for this category of wines was discussed in the chapter on fermentation, as this is a natural step in the whole procedure of sparkling wines.

BLENDING YOUR WINE
Blended wines are customary and traditional in every country and region where wine is made. The world's best wines are blends of some type or style. They could be blends of different grapes, different lots of wine, blends of the same grapes with sundry cellar treatments, grapes of the same varietal from

various vineyard plots or wines from multiple vintages. Blending wines permits the winemaker to create a better wine by assembling all the aromas, flavors and characteristics of the lots available. The blending of all the positive and, sometimes, negative attributes of wines will take practice and experience and knowledge of the components and how they will react when blended together. Before creating the final blend it is best to make small experimental lots and allow them to age for a period of time before deciding on the final wine. The possibilities are limitless, and with experimentation the results will be very gratifying.

Before the blending begins, there are many variables that should be taken into account. The winemaker should decide what the resulting wine should be and visualize and evaluate how it will look and taste to the consumer. Blending, just like a good food recipe, depends on the ingredients to be used. The winemaker should assess the wines by aroma and taste, and where necessary through laboratory analysis. These evaluations should be conducted in a clean, well-lighted environment with no aromas that could throw off the process. One might want to call in a group of friends or people whose palates you respect so that you come to a consensus opinion rather than relying on your own subjective feelings. In many commercial wineries, the final blends are made in this fashion.

Attempting to correct major flaws in wines at this point may be fruitless. High degrees of sulfur dioxide, problems of bacteria and mold infections will only ruin the blend if these wines are used. If you haven't caught these problems prior to the blending stage, it will probably be too late to correct them. Volatile Acidity (V.A.) is a flaw seen most frequently in red wines, and if the V.A. is low, you can possibly correct it by blending it with a sound wine. Try a sample blend first before creating a master blend.

Wines with very high acid can be blended with wines that could use an acid adjustment, and the resulting wine could be quite wonderful. Aromas and flavors can also be adjusted by blending. A prime example, taking into account acidity, aroma and flavor, would be the blending of Chenin Blanc and Chardonnay. This blend is practiced yearly in California. The Chenin brings a naturally high acid and delicate flavors and aromas, and the Chardonnay has very forward fruit aromas, rich body and a lower natural acidity. When combined we have a harmonious balance that will taste lovely and most consumers will think it is 100 percent Chardonnay.

Blending of wines with different cellar treatments is a fine way of combining the qualities inherent in the methods utilized. For example, you have made two lots of Chardonnay. Lot 1 was barrel fermented and had some lees aging. Lot 2 was fermented and aged in non-intrusive material with no lees aging. The rich aromas and flavors from the oak plus the slight yeastiness and complexity from the lees aging will marry beautifully with the forward fruit and delicacy of the Lot 2 wine. The Lot 2 wine may have a slightly higher acid because the barrel-aged wine may have undergone ML as well. The combination of these two treatments will add to the blend.

In Bordeaux, the Chateaux owners and winemakers have been blending wines for generations to create their elegant wines. The practice of blending different varietals can be beneficial for the home winemaker as well. It will allow you to use certain wines that alone would not make a great wine but that in combination with other lots will create something remarkable. Two grapes whose style and heritage were discussed at length in the style chapter, Cabernet Sauvignon and Merlot, make fine partners for blending purposes. Cabernet, as you will remember, has a full-bodied flavor and tannins that are quite rich, whereas Merlot is softer and more supple on the palate, and they both have similar fruit aromas and flavors. To try this in your home winery, as you check your aging lots of wine and you come across wines with these profiles, it is definitely possible that you could create a harmonious blend and finished wine.

Thankfully, aromas of wines can be altered by good blending techniques. In the instance that you have Lot 1, a white wine, which has a very vegetal aroma that is not very pleasing alone, try blending it with Lot 2, a white wine, which has very forward apple, spice and melon aromas. Hopefully the integration of the two divergent aroma profiles will give you a final blend that captures the best attributes of both lots. Some Cabernets will have very pronounced bell pepper or mint-like aromas and/or flavors. These components standing alone could be very dominant and at times unpleasant, but when blended down with a Cabernet that has cassis, blackberry, cedar and spice aromas, you can visualize how the results could be very positive and the development of aromas and flavors would be glorious over time.

In the blending of rosé and blush wines, we already know that the best way to make a good marriage is with different lots with degrees of color extraction, R.S. levels, acidity levels and even differing grape types. The final blend should be crafted using small lots of experimental batches. This holds true for all blends discussed in this book.

Another method that has been discussed is the blending of white and red wines to create a rosé/blush wine. In this case.

the blend must be made very carefully as you will be using two different wines with very divergent characteristics. The wines should be very well made and have only positive attributes to bring into the blend. There should be no glaring problems such as V.A., moldiness, sulfur dioxide or bacteria. The white wine should have nice fruit aromas and flavors, crisp acidity, a touch of R.S. possibility, and not have been aged in oak. The wines you use should stress varietal character and should also be reasonably delicate. If you are using Native American or French-American varieties, be careful about their structure, aromas and flavors. As we have learned, these varietals may have dominant components that could deter from the final blend. The reds' attributes should include good color extraction, light to moderate tannins, very little or no oak aging, forward aromas of berry fruits, no R.S. and nicely balanced acidity. The final blend should be a brilliant rosé color with a balance of all the above ingredients, no component dominating the blend, and a clean, fresh taste with good, crisp acidity. The touch of R.S. will add an attractive impression when it first hits the palate, and the crisp acidity will help to balance this touch of sweetness.

Sweet wine blending is also a nice way to balance the R.S. levels in certain lots of wine. If in your tastings during the aging process you find that you have two very distinct styles evolving, this could be the time to try a blend and see what the results might be. Lot 1 has five to six percent R.S. with nice acidity and quite forward fruit aromas, and Lot 2 about one to two percent R.S. with very zippy acidity and more restrained aromas. On paper this blend looks great, as the individual lots bring wonderful components that have a great deal in common, and the balance of aromas, flavors, sweetness levels and acidity will have an attractive interplay on the palate. In sweet wine blending it is also possible to blend different varietals. As always, be careful when choosing the lots to be blended. The hallmark of sweet wines is very forward fruit aromas, a balanced sweetness on the palate, good acidity on mid-palate and balanced sweet/acidity on the finish. Some varietals because of their dramatic components should probably not be blended for sweet wines, as they have a tendency to dominate. Experimentation is the best guide.

Please remember, after blending any wine, whether it be white, rosé, red, sweet, or sparkling, that there is a rest period needed for all the components to come together before you should consider bottling. The wines will have gone through a bit of shock and will need the time to pull all the ingredients together into a harmonious marriage. Evaluate the final blend over a period of time until you feel that the wine has pulled itself into the best condition and then begin the bottling procedure.

In conclusion, blending is an art form that both commercial and amateur winemakers continually must practice. With practice and experimentation, you will gain the knowledge and confidence necessary to craft wonderful wines that will certainly be better than if you had not blended them at all.

BOTTLING YOUR WINE

After you have completed the aging, blending, additional aging of the blend and assessment of the wine's quality, it is time to bottle your wine. What type of bottle, closure, and label design to use is a very subjective decision. There are specific sizes and shapes of bottle available that have been used for certain styles and types of wines for years. You can pick the style and shape you wish, but it is worth knowing why these shapes have been designed for the particular wines.

Bordeaux-shaped bottles are used for Cabernet Sauvignon, Merlot, Sauvignon Blanc, Semillon (dry and sweet) and wines that emulate the style of these grapes. The development of this style and shape bottle came about because of the potential aging ability of these wines, especially the red varieties. Because the wines in these bottle are closed with a cork and are aged on their sides to keep the cork moist, the very distinct style with the high shoulders was developed. The shoulders trap and keep the sediment away from the cork. This sediment will naturally occur in wines that were lightly fined (or not at all) and not filtered. This sediment may look unattractive but it signifies to wine-knowledgeable consumers that the wine is a more natural product.

Burgundy-shaped bottles are used for Pinot Noir, Chardonnay, Rhone grape varieties (Syrah, Mourvedre) and some S.B. wines that are modeled after the wines of the Loire Valley. The red varietals encased in this bottle shape seem to throw sediment that adheres to the side of the bottle. In the case of Pinot, there is certainly less sediment thrown due to its delicate color versus the deep color extraction of Cabernet.

The classic German Riesling or Hock bottle is used for Riesling, Pinot Blanc (due to its production in the Alsace region of France) and some sweet-styled wines. There are two colors available; traditionally the brown or amber color is used for wines emulating the Rhine region and the green is used for wines of Mosel-Saar-Ruwer style. Although for most people there is very little difference in these Riesling-based wines, there are slight nuances that distinguish them. For the home winemaker, these are excellent bottles to use for wines

wine bottles

German   sparkling   sparkling   Chianti

Bordeaux   Burgundy   Port   Beaujolais

that you wish to consume over a short period of time.

Champagne/sparkling wine bottles are used expressly for these wines, although many home brewers store their beer in them. The bottle style, shape and strength were developed over time, and are the only bottles recommended for this style of wine. Do not attempt to put sparkling wines in any other type of bottle. The bottles are heavier and stronger to withstand the amount of pressure created by the secondary fermentation. You will also find an indentation or punt on these bottles that is deeper than on normal bottles. This punt adds to the strength of the bottle and also allows you to pour the wine correctly.

There are many more bottle shapes and sizes made for the storage of wine, including the Chianti flask, Bocksbeutel (German Franken wines) and Beaujolais but they are not normally available to the home winemaker.

Besides your home winemaking shop, there is a new source that has become available in these times of recycling in the United States. In the past some winemakers asked their friends to save bottles for them but now there is this new source. Your friends and neighbors would rather give them to you than have them sitting at curbside. Or talk to your local recycling center about the possibility of getting bottles from them.

Many winemakers will use the jug style bottle for their everyday wines, as it is an efficient and less expensive way to store these styles of wine. The bottles have a twist top and can hold up to five or six liters of wine. These jugs are available from the supply shop and also from your friends. If you get them from a local source make sure that the screw caps work well.

Closures for wine bottles have been made predominantly

of cork. The main country for the production of high-grade cork is Portugal, where the most productive trees grow. Cork is actually a renewable resource, as the trees will rejuvenate their bark every ten to thirteen years. The cork is processed and graded for quality level and then the individual cork "basket" is formed. The remainder are regraded and used for the production of Champagne corks. This does not mean that Champagne corks are of lesser quality, only that this type of cork must be made of multiple layers of cork. The layers are formed, pressed and glued.

The quality of cork available to the home winemaker is excellent, and it is suggested that you use only the best. Using less than the best could cause leaking problems or "corked" wines. There is a trend, unfortunately, developing in the world of wines, and we are seeing more corked wines on a regular basis. The reasons for this are twofold. One is the fault of the producer of the corks who is not monitoring the corks during the drying process, and the corks are becoming infected with molds and bacteria that cause this corkiness. The second reason is the proliferation on the commercial market of cork-finished wines. Even the least expensive wines, which would have been sold with plastic or screw-cap closures, are now being sold with cork as the closure of preference. The consuming public thinks of cork as being the sign of a premium wine and looks down upon any other type of closure as cheap. Most of the wines sold with corks will be consumed within a week of purchase and certainly don't need a cork to preserve them. The easiest way to detect a "corked" wine is when you first pour it into the glass. The predominant aroma you will smell is that of wet cardboard or a musty smell. If you are unsure, take a small amount into your mouth, and if you don't perceive the normal characteristics of your wine, it is probably corked. Throw it away. Before you bottle your wines you might want to smell the new corks. If you detect any off aromas, this may be a clue to potential problems. The percentage rate for corked wines is hovering around the eight to ten percent level.

The other closures that are used include screw caps, crown caps (soda caps, used for sparkling wines), plastic tops fitted with cork underneath, plastic corks (for sparkling wines predominantly) and expansion stoppers. There is also a new type of closure in development, and experiments among commercial wineries are under way. This closure is made of cellulose fiber, and if all goes well with the market research and consumer response, it could be the replacement for cork or at the very least could take some of the pressure off the cork industry. It looks like cork and has a very similar shape and feel. The other closures mentioned above are very suitable for the home winemaker who plans to consume the wines within a short period of time. The only drawback to certain closures (screw caps particularly) is the potential for leakage depending on how these wines are stored and the length of time stored before consumption.

Depending on which bottle closure you decide to utilize, it will be wise to invest in an apparatus to aid you in placing them in/on the bottles and to give you a solid and airtight seal. Oxidation is your worst enemy, and without the proper equipment, you risk problems from this evil element of the atmosphere. A bottle corker, crown cap and Champagne corker (for sparkling wines) are essential tools for winemakers hoping for long life out of their quality wines. There are different levels of quality and price on any of these, and it is best to research the advantages, operations and disadvantages of the types prior to bottling your wines.

Preparations for the bottling of your wine will include making sure that all the equipment to be used is in sound working order, clean and sterilized (if necessary), and that the wine is ready to be bottled. The worst thing you could do to your wine after all the time and effort you have put into it is to place the wine into a situation or an environment that is not clean, to expose it to too much oxygen or to place it in a bottle that is moldy or has a bacteria problem. Your bottles should be cleaned using either an inexpensive rinser that attaches to a home spigot or with a sterilizer/rinser. You should perform this function using hot water and then let the bottles drain on a homemade rack or on the commercially available type.

Check the area where you plan to bottle the wine and insure that it is clean and void of any potential problems during the bottling. Soak the corks (if that is your closure of choice) for a few minutes in warm or hot water to facilitate the proper working of your corker. Check the wine one last time to make sure it is clear, has no faults and is at the peak of condition. If you find that after all the racking and caretaking you have spent on your wine that it is still not clear, the last-ditch effort you can make is to filter it. The process will potentially strip some of the character and components from the wine but at least it will be clear. Most basic filtering can take place using a paper sheet filtering system, which will do a nice job. There are available quite expensive pump-driven models for the serious amateur. Again, good, sound winemaking practices will certainly give you a wine that is clear enough to bottle.

Now that you are ready to bottle your wine, slowly siphon the wine through a hose into the bottle to the correct fill level. This level should allow for a small amount of air space between the bottom of the cork and the liquid. This will permit a slight expansion of the cork and proper aging of the wine. Close the bottles with your chosen closure as quickly as possible. Oxygen is your enemy, and any airborne bacteria is not helpful. If you are using a mechanical device to close the bottles (bottle corker), be prepared for the occasional accident (breaking glass) and spillage of wine; clean the area well after this occurs. Once you have finished bottling, clean the bottles of any excess wine and clean the closure equipment, the siphon, funnel and the bottling area. Any excess wine that may have ended up on the floor or anywhere else is a potential breeding ground for bacteria, molds or fungi.

After bottling, it is best to wait for a period of up to six months before drinking the wine on a regular basis. The length of time you wait will certainly depend on the style of wine and also on your patience. Be aware that just as in the blending of wine there should be a period of time for the wine to recover from the shock of bottling. Wine is a natural product and does suffer when its environment is altered or when it is moved from one container to another. Resting in a controlled climate for a few months is enough to insure that the wine is ready to be consumed. If you do decide to drink your wine soon after bottling, you will probably not enjoy it as much as you would in a few months. The aromas and flavors may be muted or altered, the acids may seem out of balance, and you may even perceive it be flawed.

Labels are a distinctive way to finish your wine and express your feelings about the wine you have created. There are many style of labels available at the supply shop, and with some research, some old wine books and a copying machine you can also design your own labels. Also, with the advent of desktop publishing and the computer age, it is possible to design your own graphically beautiful labels. You may also need to have a label gluer to apply glue, or you can apply the glue by hand to the back of the label with a small paintbrush, depending on the number of bottles to be labeled. Two other accessories for your bottles are neck labels and capsules to cover the cork. The neck label traditionally is used to show the vintage but can also be designed any way you wish. The capsules, although quite attractive, really perform no other function unless you plan to age your wine for a long period of time. They can act as an extra barrier against oxygen over time.

For sparkling wine production we have discussed the proper closures to be used; they include the cork stopper and the wire hood that encloses the cork. There are specially designed pieces of equipment for the application of each of these closures, and it is recommended that you utilize them to insure that the cork is soundly in the bottle. For sparkling wines there is also a special type of foil capsule that is designed for this style of wine and it presents a nice finishing touch to the bottle.

8
TASTING AND EVALUATING YOUR WINE

Having educated senses is the best asset you can have to insure that your wine is healthy and has an appeal to you, your family and your friends. The best education is to regularly taste your own wines, wines created by friends, and even commercial wines. This is tasting, not drinking. If you drink all the wines you may be exposed to, one, you will lose your sense of being able to judge the fine points of the wines and two, you will probably be drunk by the end of the tasting. Wine appreciation and drunkenness do not go hand in hand. Almost all wine is consumed in moderation and with food. The best sources for wine tastings or educational seminars are through your local retail wine shop or restaurants. These events vary in their scope of education and also in size. Some may be simple walk-around tastings, others will be formal lectures, and others may be dinners with foods to match the wines and a lecturer to guide you through the evening. Any or all of these will help you to build a sensory bank of information to utilize in your home winery.

The appreciation and understanding of wines brings together three of the senses, sight, smell and taste. Your eyes will give you the initial impression of color, clarity and potential sweetness level. Your sense of smell may be most important of all, as you will be able to appreciate all the beauties of the wine as well as many of the flaws. The tasting of the wine will be the final judge of its quality and whether you fully enjoy it or not.

The clarity of the wine will help you determine whether the wine was racked properly, possibly fined and filtered or if it was properly decanted off the sediment, in the case of older red wines. The color of the wine will aid you in a quick assessment of the quality and varietal or style correctness of the wine. For example, if the wine being judged is a Chardonnay, it should have a light green–gold to straw color. If the wine you are looking at has a slightly darker gold color than normal, the wine could be an older Chardonnay with some oxidative qualities or it could have been barrel-fermented in new oak with a medium to heavy toast level. Another ex-ample could be the evaluation of a Cabernet Sauvignon that you know should be a deep ruby red color with brilliant highlights. The wine poured for you has not the depth of color, but has slight fading of ruby to orange on the edge of the glass and lacks brilliance. A couple of possibilities are that is an older Cab., a Cab. that is young but was exposed to changes in temperature/sunlight, or a Cab. that is a blend of grapes and not 100 percent Cab. Your ability to understand wines by sight is very educational when it comes to judging sweet white wines. It will be able to aid you in telling if there was any Botrytis-infected fruit used and also what the poten-tial R.S. level might be. Wines with Botrytis fruit seem to have a medium to dark gold color with shimmering high-lights. As you swirl the wine in the glass, a wine with a higher level of sweetness will give an impression of viscosity. Some tasters also look at the "legs" that form in the glass. These start at the lip of the glass and stream down to the liquid. The legs help judge the richness as well as the potential alcohol level.

Aromas that emanate from the glass are considered by most professional tasters and judges as the best way to truly assess the quality of the wine, even more than actually putting the wine in your mouth. With our nose we can determine winemaking problems, fruit quality, type of fruit used, levels of sweetness and dryness, alcohol level and many other components in the wine. When evaluating the aromas of wine try to use everyday terms you are familiar with. Following are some of the descriptors that are normally used. The list of terms would take up many pages in this book, and there is a remarkable source available that was developed at the University of California, Davis Campus, called the Aroma and Taste Wheel. It is available through many fine wine shops or local wine clubs and is an exceptional guide for all wine lovers. Here is a partial list: berry fruits (cassis, blackberry, raspberry, strawberry) and the jams or preserves created from them; tree fruits (lemon, lime, grapefruit, apricot, pear, orange, pineapple); ground/vine fruits (honeydew, cantaloupe, watermelon); spices (clove, anise, nutmeg); herbs (mint, or generally fresh-cut herbs); general outdoor or household (moldy, mushrooms, fresh-cut grass, cedar, tobacco, the classic "wet dog") and the list goes on and on. As you know, none of these aromas is the source of your grape wine, but they do occur naturally through the winemaking and aging processes.

To be able to appraise the aromas that are coming from the glass, the following procedure is recommended. Pour the wine into the glass, judge the color and then give the glass a few swirls to allow the wine to breathe. Remember, it is a living thing and it does need some air for it to show its best qualities. After swirling, hold the glass up to your nasal pas-

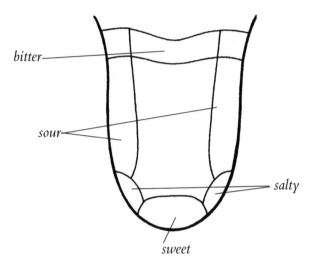

sages and breathe in. If you find that you have the glass too far away from the nose, the aromas may dissipate before you get the total effect of the wine. With some wines, holding the glass too close may be difficult, especially if they have high alcohol. If the aromas are muted, don't be afraid to swirl the glass some more. The aromas may take some time to develop, as they have been locked up for a period of time. I have seen wine aromas develop and evolve over hours in the glass. Yes, they will eventually fade as oxygen takes its toll, but the enjoyment of smelling the change is definitely worth it.

After you have finished looking at and smelling the wine, it is finally time to taste your wine. As mentioned earlier, most professionals don't drink wine, they taste it and, after evaluating it on the palate, they expectorate it into a bucket or spittoon. They will certainly consume the wine when it is served in a social setting or when it is served with food. And food is what wine was created to be consumed with, as this is when wine really shows its best qualities. To educate yourself in the best way remember the commandment: Swirl, Sniff, Taste and Spit.

When tasting wines, it is good to know the areas of your mouth and what they perceive in wine or any other product you ingest. The illustration shows the clearly defined areas in the mouth where specific nuances are felt. Thankfully with wines, there is never any salt involved so we can discount that area of the mouth. You should be aware that the so-called "cooking wine" on the shelves of your local grocery store is adulterated with salt as a preservative and should never be used by anyone serious about food and wine. At the tip of the tongue, we perceive sweetness or the lack of it in a wine. The sides of the tongue will tell us if something is sour, which in wine we know as acidity and we also perceive astringency, which is derived from the tannins in red wines. At the back of the palate we detect bitterness and also the final effects of the wine. Bitterness can come from wine that may have alcohol overpowering the fruit or other components. Alcohol is also felt as a hot sensation on the mid-palate and on the finish.

The last things you will feel in your mouth are called the finish or final impression of the wine. This is very subjective, and it comes down to whether you like the flavors, general mouth feel, acidity level, tannin level, alcohol level, fruit components and taste, whether the wine will live a long time in the bottle and what possible foods might be good to serve with it. Again, wine is a very subjective thing; don't let your palate be ruled by others unless you are a very novice taster who has asked for guidance. What you may feel is awful may be a wonderful wine to someone with a different level of knowledge and vice versus.

The procedure to use for tasting wines is as follows, with adaptations made by individuals as they learn what works best for them in the appreciation of wines. Take a small amount of wine, less than an ounce, into your mouth. As it passes over the tip of the tongue, attempt to tell if there is any sweetness. Swish the wine around in your mouth by pursing your lips and drawing a small amount of air in over the wine. If you are uncomfortable with this, just roll the wine in your mouth as you would water after brushing your teeth. This will coat the sides of the mouth and tongue and permit you to feel the effects of the wine on the middle of the palate. At this point, after giving some thought to the sensations and flavors you are tasting, spit the wine out. Then you can begin to judge the finish and the overall impression the wine leaves in your mouth and your mind. When thinking about the wine's taste, you should use the same terms that were used for the aroma section of this chapter. It is good to keep a list of these terms at hand any time you are tasting and evaluating wines. There are a few terms in tasting that you should be familiar with that don't appear when discussing aromas. Some of them are:

Attack or initial impression (this is your first reaction to the wine)
Tannin level (are the tannins balanced with the fruit?)
Acidity level (is the acidity balanced by the fruit and tannin?)
Astringency (usually comes from tannins that are very aggressive or out of balance)
Sourness (derived from wines that have high acid and possibly not enough fruit to balance)

The list could continue, but this is a good basic list. Be aware that some of these so-called problems will change as soon as you begin to serve food with the wines and also as the wines evolve in the bottle.

In conclusion, the best way to learn about wine and all its wonderful components is by tasting on a regular basis, making notes about your impressions, learning the language and putting this learning into action when assessing your own wines. Don't be afraid to ask questions.

Champagne and caviar

9
STORING, SERVING AND MARRYING WINE WITH FOOD

STORING YOUR WINES FOR AGING

Storing your wine for aging will entail some general knowledge of how the wines will age in the bottle, as well as the dedication and patience not to imbibe them before they are ready. It will also mean that you will have to set aside some space with the proper environment for the wine to age well. The information that you will gain while tasting wines with friends, colleagues and professionals will begin to help you in making the decisions necessary to choose the right wine you have made to lay down for future consumption.

Knowing which wines will age can be a difficult question to answer, and there are some general rules and guidelines that may help you in your search.

Dry white wines are thought to be very short-lived by most consumers, but in actuality many of these wines are consumed long before they should be. As we have discussed many times during the course of this book, the quality of fruit is essential to producing excellent wines. When you are making your wine and you find that the wine you have produced seems to taste and feel better on your palate and has a great finish that just goes on for ever, this might be the white wine that could do with some bottle aging. With any wine you age, balance is essential, and if there are components that stick out too much in their youth, then they will probably be more pronounced with age.

For wines produced from S.B. and Semillon grapes, what is usually desired is a balance of fruit and herbal quality on the aroma and palate, a richness in the mid-palate (whether you use oak or not, although some oak would help), crisp acidity and very good long flavors on the finish. With some bottle age of two to three years, all of the components will begin to round out and taste even better.

Chardonnay-based wines (hopefully 100 percent, and with some barrel aging) are perceived as being the only dry wines that can age gracefully. This is certainly true as long as everything is in balance (yes, balance again). Chardonnays should have attractive fruit aromas and flavors mingling with the oak qualities (caramel, vanilla, toast, etc.). When the wine is finishing on your palate, all of the qualities should be well integrated and the acidity should be pulling them all together. As the wine ages, it may take on a very rich mouth impression, the aromas and flavors will not be as forward as they once were and the acid will have softened as it becomes an integral part of the wine.

Yes, Riesling and Gewurztraminer will age beautifully. This point was reinforced on numerous occasions in blind tastings with producers in both Alsace and Germany. The two regions produce remarkable dry versions, as well as sweet versions, of these grapes. The amazing thing was the way the fruit aromas and flavors were still there but were so balanced by the now-softened acid. One would think that wines with ten to twenty years of bottle age would show a dramatic change in color, but most of these wines appeared very youthful. It can only be the quality of fruit, incredible acid balance, the winemaking practices and allowing the wine to develop its natural qualities without the aid of oak aging at all.

Red wines will definitely be the best wines to age as the fruit, tannin and acid balance is what holds these wines together for such a long period of time. Which red wines you make and decide to store will, of course, be a subjective decision, and it is suggested that you also try to be objective. It is always difficult to be objective when you are the parent of such a beautiful wine, but if all the right qualities are not there, when you open the wine in five years and all the fruit is gone and there is a screaming core of acid and tannin, you will probably regret your subjectivity.

Almost all the red wines we have discussed during the course of this book will benefit from some bottle aging. Cabernet, Merlot, Zinfandel and Syrah with their harsher tannins need the bottle age to soften and bring all the components into harmony. Varietals such as Gamay, Pinot Noir and Chambourcin may not need as much time as their tannins are generally softer and the wine is more approachable at a younger age. Whenever you are evaluating your wine keep an open mind and try to judge the wine on its positive and negative attributes. Keep in mind that the tannins, acids and fruit must work well now if they are going to age well together and taste in balance when you open the bottle in five to ten years.

Where is the best place to store your wine once you have bottled it and made that decision to age it for period of time? The best place is the same area that you aged it prior to bottling. That cool, humid and dark corner of your winery is an ideal location. If you find that you don't have the space or there is too much activity in the area, then it might be best to find some place more conducive to this long-term process.

Most wine lovers will dedicate a portion of their basement, a closet or even an old refrigerator that they will alter to suit the need. A basement is ideal, as it normally has at least three walls that are underground and this helps to control the temperature naturally. The main concerns are whether you need to insulate the walls and ceiling, put in humidity and temperature controls and what type of storage racks to use. Insulation will help in controlling the temperature and there may not be a need for other methods. Once you have found the space you want to use, monitor the environment for a period of time and see if it will work. For example, my storage area has insulation on two walls and in the ceiling, and I have three walls underground. The humidity in the room is about 50 percent year round (naturally higher in the summer), and my temperature swings from a low of 55 degrees in the depths of winter to about 68 degrees in the sweltering August heat. This is certainly not the ideal environment, but because it is a slow and gradual movement of temperature, I am not concerned that my wine is aging quickly. A neighbor has an almost perfect cellar. He dug his cellar completely underground and the humidity averages in the 60 to 70 percent range and in the summer his highest temperature has been 60 degrees. The beauty is that he accomplishes this passively with nature doing all the work. My wines are aging a bit faster than his but I am still pleased with the quality of the wines when I taste them. This commitment on your part to aging may be a bit costly, but consider that it is a one-time cost and, if you amortize it over your lifetime of enjoying wine, it will be well worth it for the pleasure that well-aged wines can bring.

The wines you store in your cellar should be laid down on their sides to keep the corks moist. The wine in contact with the cork will insure that no oxygen will come in contact with the wine due to a drying process of the cork. Also the proper humidity in the cellar will aid in keeping the cork moist. For most people, laying the wines with the label up is a general practice. It helps in identifying the wines quickly; it is also recommended that you use a secondary system to identify your wines and also to keep a cellar record. The cellar record should be for note taking and evaluating the progress of your wines, and will also be a good aid in learning which of your wines will age the best.

SERVING YOUR WINES

The serving of wine can be as simple as taking the bottle from the refrigerator, unscrewing the cap and pouring it into a glass, or it can be an involved and dramatic ritual of decanting an old bottle of red wine into a cut glass decanter, illuminating the ruby red liquid as you ever so slowly pour the wine off its sediments and pouring the wine for your guests into Reidel "Old Bordeaux" glasses. The serving of wine is fun and it is meant to be served with food, whether you are formal or casual about the procedure. It doesn't matter if the wine is young or old, inexpensive to make or the opposite. It was created to serve with food and friends. Consuming a marvelous wine should spark conversation about the wine and its merits, but it should not dominate the conversations around the table during the course of the evening. Wine is a vehicle for food and social settings, and it helps to understand the proper serving temperatures and glassware for each wine you make so that all the parts of the social gathering or casual meal will be complete.

GLASSWARE/STEMWARE

The appropriate glassware is important for the wine as well as for your appreciation of it. There are literally thousands of types, style and manufacturers of glassware available today and it will take some experimentation to find the glass that works the best for you. The basic designs have changed little over the years and these are still the best for certain styles of wine. Some manufacturers have begun to experiment and make glasses that are even more type-specific. These glasses are designed to focus the aromas properly and also to direct the wine onto the palate at the appropriate place so that you may perceive the best qualities of the wine.

The best glasses should be of the simplest and plainest design and have smooth sides, not cut glass or designs that inhibit the viewing of the wine. Most wine drinkers will find an all-purpose glass that can work with both dry white, rosé and red wines. The ideal glass should rise out gently and elegantly from the stem, have a slight pear-shaped middle and slope in gradually to the edge of the glass. This general design will allow for the aerating of the wine by swirling and will also focus the aromas nicely toward the nasal passages. A too-wide opening of the glass will let the aromas dissipate and the taster can lose some of the key olfactory beauties of the wine.

Your choice of sparkling wine glasses should not include the old standard saucer-shaped glass that was said to represent Marie Antoinette's breast. This shape does nothing for the wine and actually destroys the appreciation of the wine. The perfect glass for sparkling wines should be what is known as a tulip-shaped type. It should be quite tall and slender with a slight bowing out in the middle and tapering back in at the edge to focus the aromas. This glass will highlight the effer-

wine glasses

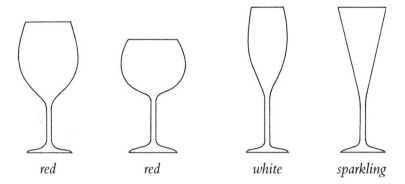

red · red · white · sparkling

vescence of the wine as it spirals upward, the delicate color of the wine (especially in Blanc de Noirs and rosé style wines) and will concentrate the bouquet towards the nose.

Dessert-style wines should be served in stemware that will hold only a few ounces of liquid and these glasses should be similar in shape to your all-purpose glass, the difference being that the opening may be a little wider at the edge. There are certain glasses designed for this purpose and also used for cognac. They work very well and are quite tapered inward at the edge of the glass, once again to focus the aromas.

SERVING TEMPERATURES

As we have learned, serving temperatures will vary with the style of wine. The myriad components will change and become more or less pronounced depending on the level of temperature of the wine. Dry white wines should be served at 45 to 55 degrees to really appreciate their complexity. Unfortunately, most restaurants store their wine with their food products because they lack the space to dedicate to wine storage.

By law, perishable products must be stored at 38 to 42 degrees, and therefore the wine you drink is to cold to show its best qualities. If you think of wine as a living entity, and that it has been locked in a container, then refrigerated at these temperatures for a period of time, it will come out of the bottle all wrapped up in itself, holding all its glories inside. When dry white wines are served in this condition, the aromas and flavors are very restrained and the acid has a tendency to be more pronounced. As the wine warms, everything begins to be more balanced and flavorful and the wine begins to breath.

Rosé and blush wines can accept a little lower temperature for serving than can dry white wines. They are meant to be refreshing and light on the palate. The wine's fruit aromas are such that the cooler temperature will not harm them much and the acids should balance well, especially on a warm summer day when refreshment is called for.

Sweet white wines should be served at 38 to 45 degrees, due to their high R.S. and their delicate acid balance. Certainly as the wine warms in the glass, the bold fruit aromas and flavors will become more pronounced, as will the sweetness level, and the acidity level will seem to retreat. Cooler temperatures also complement desserts that you might serve along with the wine.

Dry red wines are always discussed as being served at room or cellar temperature. Room temperature to us is quite different than it was back in the nineteenth century. What is cellar temperature on any given day? No matter what the answers are, it seems that the optimum temperature for red wines is between 60 and 70 degrees, depending on the time of year and time of day. Red wine aromas and flavors are closed in when too cold and the tannin levels are accentuated to the point of overpowering and sometimes deadening the palate. The exception to this rule are wines that are lower in tannin level, such as Beaujolais-style wines (Gamay grape). These wines are light, fruity and have well-integrated and light tannins and the wines actually taste great with a slight chill to them.

Champagnes and sparkling wines are served at the same temperatures as dessert-style wines. The cooler temperatures work well with the effervescence, light fruit qualities, yeast and toast-like aromas and flavors, and the crisp acidity. As the wine does warm a bit in the glass, the aromas will become more full bodied and a touch richer.

When pouring wine into the glass, do not overpour, as you want to be able to swirl the wine in the glass and permit the aromas to come out of the wine. This will also allow the taster to smell the wine properly without getting the tip of his nose wet.

As you pour the wine for your guests, hold the bottle so that they can read the label. As you finish pouring into the glass, give the bottle a quarter turn to stop any drips from precipitating from the edge of the bottle.

There is also a proper way to pour sparkling wines. The large punt at the bottom of the bottle permits you to stick your thumb in and cradle the bottle. This makes for a very elegant presentation for your guests and really showcases the wine and effort you have put into making it.

MARRYING YOUR WINE WITH FOOD

This section of the book is an area where there could actually be another book written. The food and wine scene is changing so rapidly as chefs create new dishes using unheard-of, until recently, ingredients from the far corners of the world. The popularity of Tex-Mex, Cajun/Creole, California, Spa, Caribbean/Island, French, Italian, Spanish and now middle-European cuisines has brought many new and innovative ideas to the table. This is making the marriage of food and wines more and more challenging and fun for all us willing to try and create a balanced dining experience. The old adage of "white wine with fish and red wine with meat" still holds true, but there are ways in which it is being adapted to meet the evolving food scene.

Some general guidelines are beneficial to help create well matched food and wine pairings. Acidity in wine helps to cut through the fats, proteins and carbohydrates in foods. For example, a very rich fish preparation of pan seared salmon filet with a caramelized onion sauce would be nice served with a Chardonnay partially barrel-fermented or enhanced with oak chips or Oak Mor™. The full flavors of the wine and the richness of the dish would balance each other on the mid-palate and the acidity of the wine would cleanse the mouth and set your palate up for the next bite of food. There is also the slight sweetness that occurs when you pan sear the fish. You caramelize the proteins and the fats on the exterior of the fish. Plus you have the onion sauce that adds its own sweetness from the caramelization of the natural sugar in the onion. The combination of the two types of sweetness must also be balanced and they will be by the acidity of the wine. But realize too that the perceived sweetness of the oak in the wine will combine with the sweetness in the food.

If you have a very light-styled wine, you should prepare a dish that is lightly seasoned and has a simple preparation. Consider a piece of gray sole baked in the oven with a light coating of fresh herbs and brushed with a touch of butter. Some wines you might want to try would be Sauvignon Blanc (no oak aging), Seyval Blanc or a dry to medium-dry Riesling. The herbal qualities of the S.B. and the Seyval and their naturally high and delicate acids would work wonderfully with this dish. The Riesling, with its attractive fruit factor, would counterbalance the herbal flavors from the fish and the crisp acidity would cut through the hint of fat and richness contributed by the butter. The other component to consider is the slight sweet impression from the Riesling and this would be pleasing with both the butter and the potential sweetness that derives from baking the fish.

Acids and especially tannins work extremely well to dissipate fats and proteins that are associated with red meats, some poultry and game. Red wines with most fish create a very metallic taste in the mouth, because there are not enough proteins and fats to work with the tannins. When you masticate food in your mouth, you release the fats and proteins and they coat the inside of the mouth. As the red wine enters the palate, the tannins and acids latch onto the fats and proteins and carry them into your body and leave the palate clean. This is another reason why you can drink many young red wines before they are really ready to be consumed. When you serve them with the appropriate foods to balance the high tannin levels, they will seem less tannic and more flavorful. An example would be a sirloin steak grilled to your liking with wild mushroom and peppercorn sauce. We know that the tannins will combine with the fats and proteins, but what about the earthy and spicy/hot aspects of the dish? Well, that is where the fruit characteristics come in. Red wines usually have forward berry aromas and flavors that do especially well with earth flavors and also balance the heat of the peppercorns and leave the mouth feeling refreshed.

Sweet flavors in wine make more interesting companions with dishes that have slight salty components (blue-veined cheese), sweet tastes (desserts), acid/sweet flavors (ripe fruits) and rich/sweet impressions (foie gras: fatted duck or goose liver). Sweet wines are normally served after a meal and, unfortunately, not much thought is given to how they will work with the food to accompany them. This is a shame, as sweet wine will pair nicely with many different styles of dessert foods as long as you respect the guidelines. Chocolate can be very difficult with white sweet wines and should only be matched with Ports, Madeiras and occasionally dry red wines. Yes, dry red wines. The fruit flavors of moderately tannic red wines will combine nicely on the palate with a dense chocolate dessert especially if it has a berry sauce.

When creating your menu think of the ingredients you plan to use and try to visualize how they will affect the wine you have made and also remember all the components in the wine. As we mentioned in the blending section, blending is like a food recipe, knowledge of the ingredients is essential. The manner in which you cook the food plus the ingredients used plus the components of the wine all play a particular part in the marriage of food and wines.

10
GENERAL WINEMAKING RECIPES AND PROCEDURES

WINE FROM GRAPE CONCENTRATES

Concentrates are readily available and provide the simplest and least expensive way to make wine for the amateur. They will never make great wine, due to the process and the source of the grapes. Each container is clearly marked with directions and with the additives that are in the container. The wine shop owner will be more than willing to share his expertise and knowledge about this product.

The basic instructions on a can are quite easy to follow, and therefore there is no need to give them to you here, as each manufacturer has specific ones for its brand. Most cans will contain approximately one gallon of concentrate and will yield five gallons of wine. If you wish to alter the recipe, consult the shop owner or an expert you know. If you add more water to the concentrate you will get a greater quantity of a light-styled wine. Conversely, if you reduce the quantity recommended, you will have a stronger, more full-bodied wine. Concentrates usually contain yeast, Bentonite (to prevent protein buildup and haziness), potassium metabisulfite (produces sulfur dioxide), potassium sorbate (prevents secondary yeast fermentation) and a fining agent. But each manufacturer is different and it is necessary to consult the label and the shop owner so you know how to proceed. With most concentrates, all you need is water, probably sugar and the proper fermentation equipment.

Once you have finished the fermentation, you can alter the wine. Don't waste your money on an oak barrel; use oak chips, oak essence or Oak Mor™ to add that richness. If you find the wine too flabby and lacking in acid, you can adjust it by adding an acid blend that you purchase from the shop. If you have made a red wine from concentrate you will probably have to adjust the tannin level. The best method is to buy grape tannin in granular/powder form, dissolve it in some water and blend it with the wine.

Producing wine from grape concentrate will give you the basic steps to follow and yield a palatable wine. You will be ready to move on to working with fresh grapes or fresh/frozen juices.

WINE FROM FRESH/FROZEN JUICE (MUST)
Dry White, Chard. or S.B.

You have purchased five gallons of fresh juice that is a combination of free run and light first press. It was settled and given a light or no sulfur dioxide treatment. In the case of most frozen juice you buy, it will not have been treated with sulfur, as the freezing process will inhibit any problems that might arise (spontaneous fermentation for one). The juice is very clear and free of any particulate matter and ready for fermentation to begin. You know that when the grapes were picked the brix level was between 20 and 22 degrees, the total acid was .8 percent and the ph was between 3.1 and 3.2. With these figures in hand, you know that you can produce a very high quality dry wine with a potential alcohol of ten to 12 percent. Prepare your primary fermenter and rehydrate your yeast (one packet will suffice) in water of about 100 degrees for about 20 minutes. I recommend Montrachet yeast, as it is a good yeast for this style of wine. Add the yeast and a yeast starter/nutrient, if you feel it is necessary, to the must. The must should fill the primary fermenter to about the 4/5 to 5/6 level to allow for the fermentation process action.

Fermentation should begin in about 24 to 48 hours, depending on the strength of the yeast and the temperature of the environment. Keep the temperature of the wine and the environment at about 65 to 70 degrees to guarantee a slow and even fermentation. Within ten to 14 days, the wine should be finished fermenting and should be at 0 degrees brix and totally dry. Rack the wine off the gross lees and into a clean glass carboy, add approximately 20 ppm of sulfur dioxide (if you must) and 20 grams of Bentonite (if you must) and close with an air lock. An alternative would be to allow the wine to settle for a few hours and rack it a few times rather than adding the chemicals. Remember to use an air lock at all times to inhibit the entrance of oxygen. Place the carboy or other medium (oak) in a cool dark place and allow the wine to rest, stabilize and cleanse itself for a week or more. Rack it again into a clean container and reapply an air lock. The wine should now remain in this container for up to three months. Check it regularly for problems and liquid level and top up when necessary.

If you want to enrich this wine without the cost of oak, add oak chips or Oak Mor™ after the last racking and let the wine rest in contact with the simulated oak.

The same general procedure could be used for any wine with similar characteristics. When you buy the fresh/frozen juice, find out any and all pertinent information about the wine prior to beginning the fermentation.

RED WINE FROM GRAPES, FRESH OR FROZEN
Cab., Merlot, Zin., etc.

Providing you have found a good source for fresh or frozen grapes, the winemaking process is basically the same, with some minor adjustments and some added equipment. The grapes should have been harvested at between 21 and 23 degrees brix, have T.A. of five to seven percent and a pH between 3.1 and 3.3. a 40-to 42-lb. lug box of fresh grapes will yield approximately two and one-half gallons of wine and a five-gallon pail of frozen grapes will yield a little less than four gallons of wine. If you are using frozen grapes, you will not need a crusher/stemmer but with both types of fruit you will need a grape press. As with the white frozen grapes, the reds may not have been treated with sulfur. Consult your supplier.

Make sure your primary fermenter is clean and all equipment is in good working condition. Crush and stem the grapes. If you must, treat the must (juice) with 40 to 50 ppm of sulfur and remember to keep the skins and juice in contact for proper color and phenolic extractions. Add your rehydrated yeast and nutrient (if necessary) to the must in the primary fermenter, which is about 4/5 filled. Once fermentation has begun, in 24 to 48 hours, attempt to control the temperature and maintain it in the 70-to 80-degree area. Slow and even fermenting gives you the best color extraction and will also guarantee a better wine. You will need to punch down the cap that forms on top of the fermenter two to four times per day with any clean and appropriate tool. Most people find that a sturdy wooden spoon or a high-quality potato masher works extremely well for this purpose. The cap is formed by the skins and other particulate matter rising to the top. This must be incorporated back into the fermenting juice to permit the best extraction of color and other essential components.

When fermentation has stopped, the grapes and must should be pressed very gently to obtain the optimum quality wine. A heavy pressing will only lower the quality of the wine. You should reserve the heavy pressed fractions for potential blending or for topping-up purposes. These fractions should be stored in separate containers and treated the same as the primary juice. Once you have pressed your primary wine, transfer it to a clean, fresh container (glass or oak), secure with an air lock and settle the wine for a day. Rack the wine, inoculate with a malolactic culture and fit an air lock in place.

When M.L. is finished, rack the wine again into a clean container and put it in a cool, dark and controlled environment. The wine should be checked regularly, racked occasionally, topped up when necessary and bottled when you feel it is ready. If you wanted to add the oak component to the wine without the cost of barrels, add oak chips or Oak Mor™ after M.L. has been completed and let the wine rest in contact for the desired time.

ROSÉ AND BLUSH WINES FROM FRESH/FROZEN GRAPES

Basically, you will proceed in the same manner you did for making a red wine, and you will have to monitor the fermentation and color very carefully. The length of time you leave the juice and skins in contact will vary with the grapes you use and the actual color you wish to have in the wine. Once you feel that you have reached the color you want, siphon the juice off the skins and continue the fermentation or press the juice from the skins. Realize that by pressing you will get a slightly darker wine and the flavors will be a bit more full. Finish the primary fermenting until the wine is at the R.S. level you want (hopefully below two percent and even better, dry, below .5 percent), rack the wine off the gross lees and other matter into a clean, non-intrusive vessel and put in place an air lock. Let the wine settle for 24 hours and rack again, add 20 to 30 ppm of sulfur dioxide (if you must) and about 20 grams of Bentonite (if you must) and return to a cool, dark, controlled environment for a couple of months. Monitor the progress, check for problems and bottle it when you feel it is ready.

SPARKLING WINES

The basic recipe for sparkling wines was discussed at length in Chapter 5, and you should refer back for that information.

O.H.B.'S CONCORD GRAPE WINE

I remember my grandfather talking about his experiments with winemaking, and I distinctly remember eating the Concord grapes that grew on the trellis overlooking the fields that surrounded his house. Unfortunately, I was not of legal age when he was making his wines and I never had the opportunity to taste them. He was very proper and conservative and would never consider giving wine to a minor.

Concord grapes are part of a variety of grapes known as *Vitis labrusca* (not to be confused with Italian Lambrusca wines) that are native and wild grapes. Some of them have been domesticated and were very popular as both table and wine grapes through the history of our country until the 1950's. Their popularity has been eroded by the availability of *vinifera* and

French-American hybrids for winemaking and by other varieties for eating purposes (Thompson seedless). They are still cultivated in the upstate New York grape-growing regions for grape juice (non-alcoholic) and for inexpensive jug wines. I have never made this wine, due to a lack of availability of grapes, but I have found through research that the grapes have a very poor sugar-to-acid ratio. The sugar levels tend to be quite low and the acids very high, which can make an unbalanced wine. You can certainly visualize the need to dilute and add sugar to the must to correct these problems, as you will see from the following recipe that my grandfather left me. Keeping good progress reports is essential for monitoring your wine as it evolves.

9/21 25 (approximately) pounds of Concords, 1/2 stems left on, crushed, 3+ gallons of must, add 1 quart of water and 1 cup sugar. Fermented one week.

9/27 Squeezed through a cloth bag, added one pint of water, total 2 gallons=16 pints, added 6 pounds sugar.

9/28 Skimmed solids off top

9/29   "   "   " "

9/30   "   "   " "

10/6   "   "   " " , very sweet

10/25 Racked 2 gallons and 1 quart, moderately sweet

April: (following year) A good sweet wine

May 14: Racked and bottled in quart bottles

September: Okay, still sweet but not so sweet as in April

March: (following year) Still sweet but drier than before.

No matter what my grandfathers winemaking abilities were

or his level of appreciation, to me it is his note taking and monitoring of the progress that is important for the amateur or the professional.

At this point it is prudent to discuss recipes and winemaking when using them. No recipe is foolproof, due to nature and the manner in which grapes change because of the climate and soils they are grown in. These recipes are merely guidelines, and you will hardly ever receive grapes with the exact measurements I have given. Be willing to make adjustments and alterations in the methods and process of winemaking to suit your individual needs. Experimentation has provided the advances in winemaking for centuries and it will continue long after we are gone.

SOURCES FOR WINEMAKING SUPPLIES

There are many ways to locate sources for your hobby, and one of the best places is the yellow pages of your telephone directory. Look under Winemaking/Beer Supply Shops, Vineyards, Wineries and Wine Clubs or Associations. You can also check with a good retailer of commercial wines although he is not likely to be a sound reference for this type of information. Following is a short list of some very good suppliers who will ship most of the essential equipment and ingredients you will need.

Presque Isle Wine Cellars, North East, PA.
814-725-1314
Large supplier of all types of essentials for the amateur and the small commercial winery. Will ship nationwide. Call for information and a great catalog.

Milan Laboratory and Winemaking Supplies, N.Y., N.Y.
212-226-4780
One of the oldest in the United States with large supply of essentials. Call for information and a catalog.

Arbor Wine and Beermaking Supplies, East Islip, N.Y.
516-277-3004
Good selection of essentials. Ship nationwide for most items. Call for information and a catalog.

All of the above have oak barrels for sale. Presque Isle and Arbor list only American, but Milan lists both American and French. Call for availability and shipping restrictions and costs.

CANADA:

Wine Art, Inc.
Own 21 stores throughout Canada.
Also supply 400 independent stores.
They offer a catalog as well.
Main office: 905-881-7025

UK :

The following offer both winemaking and home brewing
supplies:

The Happy Brewer
15 Union Street
MK 40255, Bedford, Shire
02-34-353-856

Cheers, Health and Homebrew
94 Priory Road
Cheam, Surrey
081-644-0934

Harvey Wine and Beer Making
174 West Street
Faireham, Hampshire
03-29-233-253

REFERENCE BOOKS FOR THE HOME WINEMAKER

The following books will give general information on wines and certain of them will be specifically about winemaking, professional and amateur. Any book you read that concerns wine will be beneficial in some fashion. If we don't learn something every day, why going on breathing.

The Wines of America, Leon D. Adams, McGraw-Hill
On Food and Cooking, Harold McGee, Charles Scribner's Sons
American Wines and How to Make Them, Philip M. Wagner, Knopf
The Book of California Wine, Muscatine, Amerine Thompson et al, University of California Press/Sotheby Publications
Vines, Grapes and Wines, Jancis Robinson, M.W., Knopf
Winegrowing in Eastern America, Lucie T. Morton, Cornell Univ. Press
The Wine Atlas of Spain, Hubrecht Dujiker, Simon & Schuster
The Wine Atlas of Italy, Burton Anderson, Simon & Schuster
The Wine Atlas Of Australia, James Halliday, Harper Collins
Progressive Winemaking, Peter Duncan and Bryan Acton, G.W. Kent Inc.
Modern Winemaking, Philip Jakisch, Cornell Univ. Press
The Art of Making Wine, Stanley Anderson and Raymond Hull, Penguin Books
Commercial Winemaking, Processing and Controls, Richard P. Vine, A.V.I. Publishing Co. Inc.
Home Winemaking from A to Z, Leo Zanelli, A.S. Barnes

If these books are not available at your local bookseller or winemaking supply shop, check the local library.

INDEX